Equilibrium business cycle theory in historical perspective

Historical Perspectives on Modern Economics

General Editor: Professor Craufurd D. Goodwin,
Duke University

This series contains original works that challenge and enlighten historians of economics. For the profession as a whole it promotes a better understanding of the origin and content of modern economics.

Other books in the series
Don Lavoie: *Rivalry and central planning: the socialist calculation debate reconsidered*
Takashi Negishi: *Economic theories in a non-Walrasian tradition*
E. Roy Weintraub: *General equilibrium analysis: studies in appraisal*
William J. Barber: *From new era to New Deal: Herbert Hoover, the economists, and American economic policy, 1921–1933*

Equilibrium business cycle theory in historical perspective

Kim, Kyun
Korea University

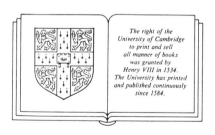

The right of the
University of Cambridge
to print and sell
all manner of books
was granted by
Henry VIII in 1534.
The University has printed
and published continuously
since 1584.

CAMBRIDGE UNIVERSITY PRESS

Cambridge

New York   New Rochelle   Melbourne   Sydney

Published by the Press Syndicate of the University of Cambridge
The Pitt Building, Trumpington Street, Cambridge CB2 1RP
32 East 57th Street, New York, NY 10022, USA
10 Stamford Road, Oakleigh, Melbourne 3166, Australia

First published 1988

Printed in the United States of America

Library of Congress Cataloging-in-Publication Data
Kim, Kyun.
Equilibrium business cycle theory in historical
perspective.
(Historical perspectives on modern economics)
A revision of the author's thesis (doctoral) –
Duke University, 1986.
Bibliography: p.
Includes index.
1. Business cycles. 2. Equilibrium (Ecomomics)
I. Title. II. Series.
HB3714.K56 1988   339.5   87–32646

British Library Cataloguing in Publication Data
Kim, Kyun
Equilibrium business cycle theory in
historical perspective. – (Historical
perspectives on modern economics).
1. Business cycles – History
2. Equilibrium (Economics)
I. Title II. Series
338.5'42'01   HB3714

ISBN 0   521   35078   6

To my parents

Contents

Acknowledgments

This book is a revised version of my doctoral dissertation, defended at Duke University, Durham, North Carolina, in April 1986. It grew out of conversations with the participants of the "History of Economic Thought" workshop at Duke. In particular, conversations with Neil de Marchi inspired me to rethink and reshape my arguments. This book would have been impossible without his urging and support. I also extend thanks to Roy Weintraub, Craufurd Goodwin, Bob Marshall, Dave Hoaas, and Jim Leitzel, who offered valuable and constructive comments. I am grateful to Colin Day, editorial director of Cambridge University Press, for his support. Finally, I acknowlege the help of my wife, Chung-Hwa, and daughter, Jihyun.

CHAPTER 1

Introduction: equilibrium business cycle theory

> [History] is a continuous process of interaction between the historian and his facts, an unending dialogue between the present and the past.
>
> E. H. Carr, *What Is History?*

In the history of economics, no subject has been more puzzling than the business cycle. Although numerous theories have been suggested since the cycle was first recognized late in the eighteenth century, none of them has succeeded in providing a full explanation of this phenomenon. The causes of the cycle suggested by these theories seem to cover every kind of economic and noneconomic factor one could imagine. Some examples may be illustrative.

Jevons (1884) firmly believed in his "scientific" explanation, according to which the fundamental cause of the business cycle lay in the periodic movement of sun spots. H. L. Moore (1914) postulated a similar "law" of economic cycles, suggesting that the rhythm of economic time series was generated by the rainfall cycle. According to Moore, the rainfall cycle was caused by the movement of Venus, which came into the path of solar radiation to the earth at intervals of eight years. Its magnetic field affected the stream of electrons from the sun and thus disturbed the magnetism of the earth and its rainfall. Hexter (1925) even claimed that the business cycle was linked to the human emotions of optimism and pessimism, which were themselves causally connected to the death of friends or close relatives and the prospect of having children; he concluded that the control of population could change the course of business cycles.

There was also a healthy skepticism about the very existence of cycles. Fisher (1925) suspected that the business cycle was an illusion, something like the cycle of luck at Monte Carlo, and called it a myth. Slutsky (1937) showed the possibility of generating business cycles by relatively simple summations and subtractions of continuous random shocks. At its most extreme, Slutsky's demonstration admitted of the interpretation that the business cycle was nothing but a statistical artifact with no substantial meaning at all.

Speculations about the business cycle, as these examples show, were wide ranging and sometimes overimaginative. Some were even too fanciful to be

1

included in the realm of pure economic thinking. As such, the business cycle was a continuing challenge to economic thinkers of the past.

Given such great efforts to solve the problem of the cycle, it is disappointing that attempts to explain it decreased rather suddenly after the Second World War.[1] Recently, however, a group of economists have challenged the old problem. Calling their theory the equilibrium business cycle theory, they are bringing business cycles back to the heart of macroeconomic thinking.[2]

The purpose of this book is to investigate the equilibrium business cycle theory from a historical perspective.[3] This chapter, as an introduction to the main work, discusses its theoretical arguments as background information for later chapters. In addition, it offers some reasons for the choice of problems to be pursued in this volume and delineates the manner in which these problems are approached. The final section provides an outline of the remaining chapters.

Equilibrium business cycle theory

Lucas's explanation of the cycle

The view that business cycles are equilibrium phenomena was not widely accepted among interwar business cycle theorists and Keynesians. With a few exceptions, such as Hayek (1933), who emphasized the incorporation of cyclical behavior into classical equilibrium theory, interwar theorists believed that cyclical fluctuations in a capitalist economy were very complex phenomena whose movements did not have a single cause or could not be easily captured by a simple theoretical framework, and certainly not by equilibrium price theory. Instead, they thought either that observed cyclical movements were a combination of several cycles (see, e.g.,

---

[1] This is not to suggest that discussion about the cycle completely stopped after the war. In fact, there arose a class of deterministic growth cycle theories, to which Hicks, Baumol, Harrod, and Goodwin, to name a few, contributed. These growth cycle theories, however, were mostly by-products of the development of economic growth theory at that time and thus were not a major current in macroeconomic thinking. For an account of growth cycle theory, see Blatt (1983).

[2] This class of theory, called here the equilibrium business cycle theory, is given different names by different writers. For instance, it has been called "new classical macroeconomics," "rational expectations economics," or "equilibrium approach to business cycles." Though each of them emphasizes different aspects, these names denote the same body of theory. In this book, the term "equilibrium business cycle theory" (EBCT) is maintained only for consistency of terminology.

[3] For a general introduction to and bibliography of the EBCT literature, see Lucas (1981), Lucas and Sargent (1981), Begg (1982), and Sheffrin (1983).

Schumpeter, 1939) or that these complex phenomena could not be explained without constructing a complex theory of cycles (see Mitchell, 1913). In contrast, the Keynesian perception of business cycles was based on the idea that the actual economy we observe is mainly a result of market failure, so that the cycle was modeled as a successive dynamic process toward an equilibrium, which is hardly justifiable theoretically and extremely difficult to achieve. For this reason, Keynesians tended to ignore the business cycle, or at best their business cycle theory necessarily produced a large and complex model, leaving an important question unanswered: Why do markets fail to sustain an equilibrium, or why does the economy successively converge to an equilibrium?

Given this pattern of development of business cycle theory, it is quite remarkable that the equilibrium business cycle theory (EBCT), pioneered by Lucas, attempts to revive the equilibrium doctrine that was not accepted as a principle of modeling cycles by either Keynesians or most interwar theorists.

"Equilibrium" simply means that every agent in a decentralized market economy chooses his behavior so as to optimize his objectives given his constraints. The rational expectations hypothesis is an application of the optimization principle to a situation in which agents face uncertainty about future events and form expectations using the information available to them; it is a hypothesis about how expectations are formed in the most efficient way, that is, a hypothesis that the subjective expectations of an agent are equivalent to the mathematical expectations conditional on a given information set. In the case of linear models, rational expectations turn out to be equal to the least squares estimator. Therefore, it can be said that the rational expectations hypothesis is an extension of static Walrasian equilibrium theory, wherein an agent's optimization problem is essentially timeless, to the dynamic equilibrium, wherein the agent's planning horizon in his optimization problem is in principle infinite in time. In a macroeconomic context, this equilibrium doctrine implies that aggregate fluctuations should be consistent with the optimizing behavior of individual agents, provided that there is no serious aggregation problem. In other words, there should not be a contradiction between microeconomic behavior and macroeconomic phenomena, which had been a puzzle for Keynesians.

Under this relatively simple principle, the EBCT has theoretically elucidated important features of cycles, such as comovement among different time series, and has eliminated the Keynesian's ad hoc[4] assump-

---

[4] Lakatos (1970) distinguishes three different concepts of ad hocness. In contrast to the traditional Popperian notions of ad hocness, what he calls ad hoc$_3$ characterizes a theory that is obtained through a modification of auxiliary hypotheses that

tions, which have no foundation in optimization but are employed only to fit the observed data. Relying on a smaller set of principles than earlier theories, the EBCT represents an attempt to explain the facts that have puzzled Keynesians and thus to achieve scientific progress.

In his seminal papers, Lucas suggests the EBCT as a new approach to the business cycle (see Lucas, 1973, 1975, 1977). He views the business cycle as a reflection of the optimizing behavior of agents in a situation of incomplete information. In his model economy (the "island economy" fable),[5] an agent is isolated in his own market; he can precisely observe this market in which he participates, but he does not know what is currently happening in other markets. Except for this current information about other markets, an agent's information set includes the history of the entire economy and local elements such as changes in tastes and technologies, that is, his utility function and production function. In equilibrium, the state of this economy can be described by a set of relative prices. These prices carry to agents all relevant information, such as quantities and changes in tastes and technology, so that an agent's information set can be reduced to the history of prices in all markets and the current local price in his own market.

An agent, who does not have access to current relative prices (real wages), has to form expectations about the current economy-wide price level in order to make the work-leisure decision that depends on relative prices (real wages) using his information set and his knowledge of the economic structure.[6] If he guesses that the current price level is favorable to him, that is, if he perceives from the rise in local price that the structure of relative prices has changed in a way that is favorable to him, he will work

do not accord with the heuristic of the scientific research program. In the context of economics, Hands (1985) observes that recent theorists, in particular new classical economists, tend to use the term for theories not derived from individuals' optimizing behavior. That is Lakatosian ad hoc$_3$ness. In most cases in this book, the term implies this ad hoc$_3$ness, unless otherwise indicated.

[5] The "island economy" fable was originally that of Phelps (1970).

[6] Instead of contemporaneous substitution, the intertemporal substitution setup is another way of deriving the "Lucas supply function." Barro (1981) stresses the legitimacy of the intertemporal substitution approach for modeling the business cycle. In that case, agents will compare current local prices with expected future price levels. A change in intertemporal relative prices will induce agents to reallocate their labor supplies intertemporally. But this setup has some unclear aspects, such as its somewhat unrealistic intertemporal substitution of leisure and the assumption that the income effect does not dominate the substitution effect. In short, the question is whether the intertemporal substitution effect could solely account for historically observed volatile fluctuations in employment time series.

more, enjoy less leisure, and produce more. This is the story described by the "Lucas supply function,"[7] which establishes the comovements among price, employment, and output during the cycle.

Models similar to Lucas's, in which only unexpected price changes have an effect on output, were suggested by Friedman (1968) and Phelps (1970). Friedman, for example, postulates asymmetric information between producers and workers, and demonstrates short-run Phillips trade-offs but a vertical long-run Phillips curve. Friedman's model is virtually identical with Lucas's, except that Friedman uses the adaptive expectations formation. Like Lucas, he understands the short-run Phillips trade-off basically as a matter of information. During price fluctuations, workers cannot observe the economy-wide price level that is necessary for calculating their real wage, whereas producers do not need information on the price level because, for them, the prices of their products are the only information necessary for calculating real wages in their labor demand schedule. The workers' misperception of the price level leads to an incorrect work-leisure decision and thus to output fluctuations. Thus, Friedman's idea differs little from Lucas's EBCT, in the sense that in both cases the observed short-run Phillips trade-offs are viewed as trade-offs between unexpected inflation and output, caused mainly by an information deficiency.[8]

Lucas then introduces money as a source of price movements. The view that the monetary phenomenon is the main source of business cycles in a capitalist economy has been maintained by Hawtrey, Hayek, Fisher, and monetarists. Lucas follows this tradition. In his island economy, however, agents who know the working of this economy (including both the way money is generated and the neutrality of money), but who do not know the current level of money stock, utilize the movement of money to form expectations of the current price level. The result is the well-known proposition that the systematic part of money put in the economy has no effect on output and is fully reflected in the movement of the price level,

---

[7] By explicitly introducing the capital market in this economy, i.e., by postulating that what agents care about is the relative real rate of returns instead of relative prices, the Lucas supply function could be modified to include interest rates. Barro's (1981) approach would be an example of such a modified version. But even in this case, the results of this model would not be changed if one assumed that real interest rates are constant or independent of price movements. See Lucas and Rapping (1969).

[8] Gordon (1981) points out that the term "Lucas supply function" is misleading. He prefers "Friedman supply function." Indeed, Friedman's (1968) presidential address to the American Economic Association was published while Lucas and Rapping were working on the paper (1969) in which they introduced the Lucas supply function in an explicit form. See Lucas (1981, esp. the Introduction).

because it does not change the structure of relative prices, which is the only variable agents care about. Only the unsystematic part of money, which agents cannot successfully predict, affects output by creating a price surprise that forces agents to reevaluate their work-leisure decision. In short, cycle phenomena are generated by agents' misperception of relative prices, and the main cause of the cycle is money. In this way, Lucas explains one of the fundamental features of the business cycle – the procyclical movements of money, price, and output.

Central components of the EBCT

The EBCT has three fundamental components: (a) an optimization foundation in a general equilibrium context, (b) the natural rate hypothesis, or the neutrality of money, and (c) the incomplete information assumption.

The most distinguishing feature of the EBCT is that its modeling strategy is based on optimization[9] in a framework of general equilibrium.[10] To see this, consider an economy in which every agent optimizes his objective, taking into account the environment, such as the behavior of the other agents (e.g., the government) and the structure of the economy (e.g., tastes and technology). One way of describing such an economy is to define "equilibrium" as functions of environments. Then equilibrium prices will be a function of tastes, technologies, policy rules, and so on. Choice

[9] The notion of *market clearing* should be distinguished from the *optimization foundation*. Market clearing does imply an optimization foundation, but not the other way around. As Mishkin (1983b) emphasizes, non-market-clearing models can also incorporate the optimization foundation. Institutional factors, such as transaction costs, cost of collecting information, and moral hazard problems, can be barriers to market clearing in spite of the optimization behavior of agents who do not leave out unexploited gains from trade. Probably for this reason, Lucas and Sargent (1978) also distinguish these two notions.

[10] Hoover (1984), contrasting the New Classical economics of Lucas with the monetarism of Friedman, emphasizes the general equilibrium aspects of New Classical economics, which are significantly different from Friedman's partial equilibrium approach. Accordingly, he labels Friedman a Marshallian and Lucas a Walrasian. Also see Weintraub (1985), who classifies the EBCT as theory in the protective belt of the neo-Walrasian research program. According to Weintraub the EBCT's hard-core proposition is, in a Lakatosian sense, the optimization principle, which is also the hard-core proposition of the neo-Walrasian research program. The rational expectations hypothesis is nothing but a direct derivation from the optimization principle extended to the problem of expectations of future events.

functions, which are observable, are also functions of such environments. If the environment changes, equilibrium prices and choice functions will also change.

This is the idea of the Lucas critique of macroeconometric models (Lucas, 1976). If some part of the environment changes, he argues, a model constructed on the basis of observable choice variables is no longer valid. Coefficients of this model are not invariant under environmental changes, because agents react to these changes and behave differently than they did in the past. In this sense, the EBCT follows the general equilibrium approach. The partial equilibrium approach, in contrast to the general equilibrium approach, assumes that changes in the environment have no effect on the particular choice function under consideration. Even conventional simultaneous-equation econometric models, which pretend to adopt the general equilibrium approach, follow this partial equilibrium approach implicitly when assuming that the coefficients of the individual behavioral functions in the system are stable. Conventional macroeconometric models thus cannot be used safely for the purpose of forecasting effects of policy. A change in a policy rule results in corresponding changes in the coefficients in the system.

A natural way of avoiding the Lucas critique is to find "deep" parameters of tastes, technology, and so on, that are believed to be invariant to changes in the environment. That is to say, the strategy of econometric modeling of the EBCT is to formulate explicitly the agents' optimization problem and the policy variables and derive from this setup their behavioral equations, which are observable and are the function of tastes, technology, and policies. Thus, by connecting these deep parameters to observable variables theoretically, econometricians can construct the "cross-equation restrictions" that account for changes in the environment (see Sargent, 1981). If the policy regime changes, the cross-equation restrictions, which link the observable behavioral equations to policy variables, would require the coefficients to change in the behavioral equations. Econometricians then could test the cross-equation restrictions in their empirical work. But empirical testing presents certain difficulties: It is hard to find the policy regime changes,[11] and the results of empirical testing are very sensitive to the way in which the optimization problem is set up.[12]

[11] Lucas (1973) uses cross-country data to get around this difficulty.
[12] Geweke (1984) shows several examples of the sensitivity of the Lucas critique to the selection of representative agents and aggregation across prices. He seems to argue that the fundamental difficulty with the EBCT's econometric modeling strategy lies in the very fact that this strategy emphasizes the representative agents at a very micro level, but uses aggregate macro data. Criticisms of the EBCT's econometric strategy are discussed in depth in Chapter 5.

It is worth noting that the EBCT adheres to the natural rate hypothesis. According to the EBCT, changes in tastes and technology cause the real economy to fluctuate. (This can be interpreted as the natural rate.) Money is then superimposed onto the fluctuations. This monetary impulse generates further fluctuations of the economy. The critical point here is that the natural rate hypothesis is distinct from the optimization principle or the rational expectations hypothesis. The famous "policy ineffectiveness proposition" (Sargent and Wallace, 1975) is a theoretical demonstration that is possible only when these two hypotheses are jointly applied. Without the natural rate hypothesis, the policy ineffectiveness proposition does not necessarily hold. In this regard, the Fisherine tradition, reevaluated by Friedman (1968), is well accommodated by the natural rate hypothesis. If real interest rates are determined independently of monetary movements or if they are determined by tastes such as "time impatience," then the natural rate hypothesis will hold. Thus, empirical evidence for the Fisherine theory would be crucial for establishing the validity of the natural rate hypothesis and the policy ineffectiveness proposition (cf, Grossman, 1983).

Finally, an essential assumption of the EBCT, contrary to that of the classical tradition, is that information is not perfect. This assumption per se is consistent with traditional economic theory in the sense that information has to be treated as a scarce commodity; the profound impact of this assumption, however, stems from the fact that incomplete information can provide the theoretical justification for error terms, such as the measurement error or the specification error, that used to be employed for statistical reasons. If the world perceived by agents is uncertain, then the model should express this characteristic of the world in some way. One obvious way might be the introduction of errors in the agents' perception of the world. And the introduction of incomplete information necessarily makes the theory stochastic and dynamic.[13]

When this internally coherent theory, like the general equilibrium theory in its heyday, was introduced to the profession, some regarded the EBCT as a revolutionary advance in economic theory. However, it has also received diverse criticisms. Among them, Tobin (1980) cites the market-clearing assumption, the problematic formulation of rational expectations, the lack of a learning process, the aggregation problem, and the serial correlation problem. His criticisms are leveled mainly at the EBCT's assumptions, except that of serial correlation. If one follows Friedman's (1953) famous

---

[13] It is dynamic by virtue of the fact that it introduces expectations formation. If information were perfect, agents would have no need to form expectations about the future or anything else. Thus, under conditions of perfect information, the agent's optimization problem is static, and so is the theory.

instrumentalistic methodology, what matters is not assumptions but predictions. Thus, assuming that equilibrium business cycle theorists accept the Friedman methodology,[14] it would not be a direct criticism of the EBCT that its assumptions are unrealistic. For equilibrium business cycle theorists, the most serious criticism would be that their theory could not provide an explanation of the serial correlation of economic time series, while at the same time eliminating ad hoc assumptions and respecting the principle of optimization.

Real business cycle theory

A widely accepted definition of business cycles is that of Burns and Mitchell (1946):

Business cycles are a type of fluctuation found in the aggregate activity of nations that organize their work mainly in business enterprises; a cycle consists of expansions occurring at about the same time in many economic activities, followed by similarly general recessions, contractions, and revivals which merge into the expansion phase of the next cycle; this sequence of changes is recurrent but not periodic. (p. 3)

In short, business cycles could be defined as phenomena of comovements and recurrences among aggregate time series. An important point is that, mathematically, this recurrence property of cycles can be generated by low-order random or stochastic difference equations (see Sargent, esp. ch. 11). That is, the low-order serial correlation of errors is the mathematical expression of recurrences of cycles.[15] This suggests that the failure to justify the serial correlation of forecasting error or the persistence effect of individual series directly implies that the EBCT could not successfully account for the recurrence property of cycles.[16]

[14] The only methodological statement by equilibrium business cycle theorists is that of Lucas (1980). Lucas emphasizes that the realistic artificial model is not necessarily superior to the unrealistic one; on the contrary, in most cases the unrealistic model has potential usefulness for thinking about reality. This sort of view, which is analogous to that of Simon (1969), has some flavor of the Friedman methodology.

[15] An equation with a serially correlated error term can be easily transformed into a stochastic difference equation. An equation with a first-order serially correlated error term, for example, is equivalent to a first-order stochastic difference equation with white noise that has a lagged dependent variable term in its right-hand side.

[16] Sargent (1979) gives an example of generating a form of business cycle by a second-order stochastic difference equation. Citing Granger (1966), who reports that the estimated power spectra of typical seasonally adjusted economic time series have a monotonically declining shape from the left to right, Sargent discusses the possibility of generating processes that resemble business cycles by

Acting on this criticism, equilibrium business cycle theorists have tried to incorporate serial correlation into their model. According to the EBCT, if the agent's information set includes the history of the variable being forecasted (i.e., prices), then the forecast errors should be serially uncorrelated. In other words, the agent's forecast error in this period should not be systematically connected with the forecast error in previous periods. If an agent commits a systematic error, he apparently violates the rational expectations hypothesis. Because he does not fully exploit the information available to him and leaves some part of it untouched, his expectations cannot be carried out in the most efficient way. Therefore, the only situation in which rational agents permit systematic errors is one in which their information sets do not include the complete history of previous prices. This situation could exist if "the price indexes appropriate to agents' decisions are never collected, so that the published price indexes are error-ridden" (Sargent, 1979, p. 331). But it is not at all realistic to attribute the serial correlation or the cyclical fluctuation of aggregate time series solely to the deficiency of published data.

Another way of looking at this problem is to distinguish sources of impulses from propagation mechanisms (Lucas and Sargent, 1978). This distinction has been known to econometricians since Slutsky (1937) and Frisch (1933) first pointed it out.[17] The idea is that it enables one to construct propagation mechanisms that convert impulses into serially correlated movements, while still keeping impulses serially uncorrelated. This simple idea is the starting point of the real business cycle theory. This is an effort to construct such propagation mechanisms that enable one to explain the serial correlation of the cycle, while maintaining the optimization principle of the EBCT. This theory is also a successor of old business cycle theories that postulated real sectors of the economy as the cause of cyclical fluctuations.

The modeling strategy of the real business cycle literature follows the one developed by the EBCT. It starts with an individual agent who optimizes his behavior under uncertainty. For instance, consumers maximize their expected utility function, which specifies their current and future preferences for commodities and leisure. A firm's production technology is characterized by a standard production function, which assumes positive

constructing low-order stochastic difference equations even though their power spectrum does not reveal a peak in the business cycle range. A downward-decreasing spectrum is a characteristic of highly, positively, low-order serially correlated time series. Thus, it is, at least mathematically, possible that even the first-order stochastic difference equation can capture the main feature of cycles.

[17] The historical development of the idea of the impulse and the propagation mechanism is dealt with in more depth in Chapters 3 and 4.

and diminishing marginal productivity in its arguments. Moreover, this production process can be subjected to technological shocks. This sort of setup is identical to Lucas-type models. Some propagation mechanisms are then introduced by modifying the utility function or production technology, or the monetary and financial system can be introduced as the additional propagation mechanism. The most critical aspect of the real business cycle theory, which might be an important deviation from the EBCT, is that it can mimic the main features of business cycles without necessarily introducing money. Because whatever the initial impulses are, propagation mechanisms are responsible for the generation of cycles; money is not necessary in this scheme. Money can be the initial impulse, but it can also be a real shock (such as a technology shock). Thus, the Lucas-type model, in which a monetary shock is the "force triggering the real business cycle" (Lucas, 1977, p. 233) becomes less compelling.

Another interesting implication of the real business cycle theory is that observed business cycles are not deviations from natural rates and their fluctuations are a course that satisfies the optimality property of a Walrasian economy.[18] Under the Lucas-type EBCT, which does not introduce the propagation mechanism, observed fluctuations are deviations from natural rates, and fluctuations directly imply welfare losses. In this regard, the real business cycle theory might further enhance the equilibrium approach to business cycles.

Although diverse propagation mechanisms are introduced in the real business cycle literature, the common theme is that produced inputs and interrelation between sectors are important for understanding the persistence and comovement of time series (King and Plosser, 1984). In a sense, this is a revival of the old view that complex structures or institutions of the market economy are responsible for economic fluctuations.[19] The propagation mechanisms proposed in the literature thus far can be categorized as (a) agents' response patterns to real shocks, (b) time-spending characteristics of production processes, and (c) monetary institutions. Long and Plosser (1983) emphasize intratemporal and intertemporal substitutions of consumer preferences and production possibilities. "At given prices, . . . consumers want to 'spread' any unanticipated wealth increment over both time and commodities" (p. 41). The spread over time causes serial correlations, and the spread over commodities is responsible for comove-

---

[18] Long and Plosser (1983) suggest this strict interpretation by examining a business cycle model with perfect information. Even with incomplete information, however, their interpretation is still valid. See also Grossman and Weiss (1982).

[19] For the old view, see Haberler (1963, esp. pp. 461–7.)

ments. Similarly, production is carried out by the employment of a variety of produced inputs, and each commodity is assumed to have many alternative uses. In other words, each commodity has a large range of intratemporal and intertemporal substitution opportunities. Given these circumstances, if the range of substitution opportunities is large enough to overshadow relative price adjustments, an unexpected shock in the production process, for example, might lead agents to choose a plan that generates features of business cycles.

Kydland and Prescott (1982) present a business cycle model based on the assumptions of multiperiod construction and the non-time-separable utility function.[20] They emphasize the relative importance of the multiperiod construction assumption in explaining the observed persistence of output, compared with the conventional adjustment cost explanation of the persistence effect.

King and Plosser (1984) present a model that includes the financial industry and generates comovements among money, price, and the real economy. The distinguishing feature of their model is that economic institutions, such as financial systems, or government regulations can be propagation mechanisms. The idea is that the output of the financial industry (transaction services) is an intermediate good that is used by firms and households. Thus, an increase in output induces credit expansion, and there will be a positive correlation between inside money and output.

This "inside money" idea, however, is strictly opposed to the exogeneity of money and leads to doubts about the monetary explanation of cycle fluctuations in which money is the prime cause. In a sense, the unsettled problem of identifying the causes of business fluctuations, which was the serious concern of interwar theorists, has been revived in the real business cycle literature.

The EBCT explanation of business cycles as an outcome of the optimization behaviors of agents in situations of incomplete information contributes to our understanding of business cycles. It emphasizes the importance of information in business fluctuations and demonstrates that optimization behavior, or the notion of equilibrium, is not necessarily in conflict with cyclical fluctuations.

---

[20] Kydland and Prescott (1982) use a form of the non-time-separable utility function. In addition to its computational convenience, the advantage of using this class of utility function instead of the time-separable utility function is that it admits greater intertemporal substitution of leisure. It could be justified by a Beckerian household production theory (Kydland and Prescott, 1982), but there is no empirical or theoretical agreement among researchers as to its particular form.

In the light of the history of business cycle theories, however, the earlier Lucas-type EBCT, which views the movements of money as the fundamental cause of business cycles, is a successor of the interwar monetary cycle theory and monetarism. The natural rate hypothesis is fully adopted, and Friedman's basic argument on economic policy is reinforced by the EBCT. But like monetarist theory, the Lucas-type EBCT is unable to explain the recurrence of cycles. Subsequent real business cycle theories have successfully demonstrated the propagation mechanisms that generate major characteristics of cycles, such as comovements and recurrences, without undermining the EBCT's optimization foundation. In addition, these real business cycle theories require the revision of the idea that monetary fluctuation is the prime cause of business cycles and invite the rediscovery of the diverse interwar cycle theories. This is so because the propagation mechanisms in the real business cycle model could be either financial systems or production processes or other elements of the economic structure that were already well understood by interwar theorists. Thus, if real business cycle theory is taken seriously, and if it is conceded that the economic structure itself generates cyclical movements, then monetary movement is of secondary importance for understanding cycles. Accordingly, this even weakens the theoretical foundation of the EBCT's policy claim that monetary policy should follow a fixed rule.

Therefore, the trouble with real business cycle theory is that, although it presents diverse mechanisms that propagate the initial shock and generate cyclical fluctuations, none of them is absolutely preferable to the others. Each has its own plausibility, but a comprehensive and fully acceptable picture of the propagation mechanism has not yet been suggested. This might be another piece of evidence for the familiar argument that our concrete knowledge about the working of the economy is not sufficient to construct a reliable theory. And this alone would be reason enough to look back at the rich discussions about the cycle that took place in the interwar years. One purpose of this book is to undertake such an exploration.

The setting of the problem

As discussed in the preceding section, a fundamental principle of the EBCT is that of optimization. This theorizing principle creates two important and inseparable features of the EBCT, each of which is very distinctive in light of the history of business cycle theory.

First, it portrays the business cycle as an equilibrium phenomenon. That is, cyclical fluctuations are not a consequence of individual agents' failure to coordinate their optimizing behavior, but rather are a result of their optimal choices. Therefore, according to the EBCT, cyclical movements of economic time series are equilibrium paths that reflect individuals' voluntary and optimal choices.

Second, the EBCT does not allow econometric models to deviate from theoretical models. Econometric modeling should be subordinated to economic theory by means of strict theoretical restrictions. The frequent presence of "free parameters" in conventional econometric models, which are introduced only to rationalize the data at hand and have little theoretical significance, is not desirable, since there is no theoretical reason to expect these free parameters to remain invariant beyond sample points. Furthermore, when theoretical restrictions are tightly connected with the optimization principle, that is, when the econometric model composed of observable behavioral equations is derived from individuals' dynamic optimization problems, the parameters in the behavioral equations of the econometric model come to be linked to the "deep parameters" of such state variables as tastes and technology. The resulting system, then, should be invariant in the face of changes in the environment, once the deep parameters are discovered.

These two distinctive features of the EBCT, in a sense, can be considered to be new solutions to old problems. Throughout the long history of business cycle theory, the phenomenon of the cycle was perceived to be strong empirical evidence against the validity of classical equilibrium theory, and business cycle theories were even regarded as attempts to replace the tradition of classical theory. It was the Austrian economists of the interwar period, however, who questioned the idea of so deep a cleavage between business cycles and equilibrium theory. Hayek, Mises, and to some extent Schumpeter and Morgenstern would be included in this tradition. Unlike other cycle theorists, the Austrians always placed the problem of incorporating business cycles into equilibrium theory at the heart of their theoretical efforts. Austrian cycle theory, though short-lived, is a product of their struggle with this problem. It might be reasonable to speculate, in this context, that the problem the Austrians attacked is the same one that today's EBCT accepts as its starting point, although the Austrians' solutions to the problem are somewhat different from those of the EBCT.

The second distinctive feature of the EBCT, its econometric strategy, can also be historically understood as a new type of solution to an old problem – that of discovering a true or stable structure by means of econometric tools. During the early phase of the econometric movement, in which new statistical techniques were intensively introduced into economics and the field called econometrics was created within the economics discipline, this problem was attacked from various perspectives. Given the two possible sources of acquiring economic knowledge, *a priori* reasoning and empirical data, some chose the former, pointing out the fundamental deficiency of economic data and the inadequacy of statistical techniques for dealing with the intrinsically complicated nature of economic phenomena. Most cycle theorists adopted this stance. But there were also statisticians who distrusted the body of economic theory and tried to discover a true system by scrutinizing the empirical world without the help of theory.[21] In between these rather extreme positions, a group of econometricians, later identified with the Cowles Commission method, believed that *a priori* theory should play an active role in the search for a true econometric structure.

These discussions on the fundamental problem of econometrics in the early econometric movement were somehow resolved into the Cowles Commission method, which was constructed mainly by Haavelmo and Koopmans. In retrospect, the original research program of Haavelmo and Koopmans, though it was later seriously twisted by the tendency toward large-scale econometric modeling in the 1960s, seems to share the spirit and methodology of today's EBCT. Both emphasize the role of theory in econometric practice and deny a purely empirical approach. A main difference between them, however, lies in their attitude toward theory. Whereas today's New Classical economists firmly believe that equilibrium theory, based on the optimization principle, should be *the* theory that commands and restricts the econometric model, the original Cowles Commission program is not as adamant about this matter.

The econometric approach to business cycles, which underlies the EBCT's theoretical structure, emerges as an important historical issue. Historically the econometric approach in the 1940s would be interpreted as an effort to quantify descriptive interwar cycle theories. As is always the case in the quantification or mathematization of descriptive theory, however, the process of adopting the econometric approach has resulted in both a loss of some theoretical contents and a change in the meaning of some fundamental concepts in interwar cycle theories. Rich verbal discussions in the interwar years about capital goods and money, for instance, could not be successfully translated into econometric language. And the econometric approach helped to change the notion of cycles: The traditional concept of cycles, constituted in terms of the wavelike characteristics of economic time series, became weaker and cycles came to be conceived simply as a special case of economic fluctuations; thus, the characteristics of cycles associated with their recurrence tended to be ignored in the study of cycles. In this vein, the formulation of the econometric approach not only was a moving

---

[21] See, e.g., Mills (1924), who preferred statistical induction to deductive reasoning as a scientific method.

force in the history of cycle theory, but provides a critical clue for understanding the very foundation of the contemporary manner of modeling business cycles.

The main purpose of this book is to enhance our understanding of today's EBCT, on the one hand, and interwar business cycle theories and the early econometric movement, on the other, by means of a historical comparison of these distinct bodies of theory. By choosing as one's starting point the problems with which contemporary theory starts, one might see the past differently and understand it better, since knowledge of the contemporary way of addressing the problems at hand provides a firm criterion for disentangling the somewhat complicated ways of thinking of the past. At the same time, it is hoped that an understanding of past economic thinking will provide a better understanding of the state of contemporary theory— even more so if one believes that the state of today's theory is in some ways unsatisfactory.

More specifically, considering the diversity of theories about the approaches to the phenomena of cyclical fluctuations during the interwar period, it would be extremely difficult to disentangle those theories and approaches without a solid criterion or perspective. If one adopts as a criterion a retrospective perspective in which interwar economic thinking is molded into the frame of today's EBCT, the interwar period can be interpreted as one that challenged the problems of both incorporating the phenomenon of the cycle into equilibrium theory and quantifying descriptive cycle theories. Then it becomes possible to make some direct comparisons between the EBCT and the interwar economic thinking, and the historical development of such fundamental concepts in the EBCT as the misperceived price information, expectations, individuals' optimizing behavior, and cross-equation restrictions can be better understood. Furthermore, this historical approach suggests that the real content of the EBCT is no richer than that of interwar cycle theories in the sense that it does not contain some well-established aspects of the cycle such as maladjustment in capital goods and that its econometric strategy is an extreme version of the Cowles Commission method and thus cannot escape the criticism to which the latter is vulnerable.

Organization of the book

Chapter 2 discusses the relationship between business cycle theory and classical equilibrium theory from a historical perspective. The first genuine effort to incorporate business cycles into equilibrium price theory was made by Austrian business cycle theorists in the interwar years. Focusing on

Hayek's theory of cycles, it is shown how Hayek attempted to fill the gap between business cycles and equilibrium theory. This chapter might also be regarded as a historical study of economic theory between the wars, a marvelous period that is still awaiting appraisal by historians of economics.

Chapter 3 traces the early econometric movement in the 1930s and 1940s. Struggles with the stability of the econometric structure are discussed in the context of a review of different approaches to the problem and a variety of views on econometrics. The emphasis, however, is on the original Cowles Commission method, established mainly by Haavelmo and Koopmans in the early days of the commission. Along with this, econometricians' unsuccessful attempts to understand the business cycle through econometric reasoning – the econometric approach to business cycles – are discussed in this chapter. It is suggested that Frisch's scheme of distinguishing the propagation mechanism and external impulses provided theoretical momentum both to the econometric movement and to the formulation of the econometric approach to business cycles.

Chapter 4 presents historical comparisons between the EBCT and interwar cycle theories as well as the early econometric movement. Here, Hayek's work is compared with today's equilibrium approach to business cycles, and Haavelmo and Koopmans's original research program is contrasted with the econometric strategy of the EBCT. These historical comparisons give rise to the suspicion that economic theory might have lost its real content in the name of formal rigor in theorizing and that our understanding of economic phenomena cannot be said to have increased, at least in the case of business cycles.

Chapter 5 pairs with Chapter 3 and surveys the contemporary trends of macroeconometrics. Three major currents of econometrics – the New Classical approach and the approaches of Sims and Hendry – are discussed. The tensions between them seem to parallel those in the 1940s between the Cowles Commission, on one hand, and the National Bureau of Economic Research and Friedman, on the other. This revival might imply at least that the old problems have not yet been completely solved and that we are still struggling with them.

Chapter 6 presents a summary of the book and some concluding remarks. It suggests that more research on the historical processes of mathematization and quantification of economic theory is not only desirable for its own sake, but necessary for a clear understanding of interwar-period theories.

CHAPTER 2

The classical tradition and business cycle theory

Although the phenomenon of the business cycle was recognized in the early nineteenth century, it was not an independent subject of study. It was neglected by most classical economists, and business cycle analysis was continued largely by economic writers outside the classical tradition, especially in the nineteenth century.

The turn of the century, however, gave way to a different phase of cycle studies. A seeming contradiction between classical theory and the cycle phenomenon began to be recognized; rather serious efforts to incorporate the business cycle into equilibrium followed. Hayek (1933, 1935) is a leading example of an economist who made this effort. Hayek's theory, as it turned out, was an unsuccessful competitor of Keynesian economics, which had replaced classical theory; nonetheless, Hayek's business cycle theory deserves credit in that it was the first systematic attempt to include the phenomena of business cycles in the territory of classical economics. In other words, his cycle theory was different not only from classical theory, which regarded the business cycle as an unimportant temporary phenomenon, but also from Keynesian economics, which in fact left behind classical thinking and asked a fundamentally different set of questions, having chiefly to do with unemployment.

In this chapter, the main concern is the attempt by interwar business cycle theorists to incorporate business cycles into classical equilibrium economics. This seems especially important once one takes account of the fact that the recent equilibrium business cycle theory is claimed to be a successor of interwar cycle theories. The chapter comprises three sections. The first deals with business cycle theories in the nineteenth century.[1] The

---

[1] Classification of business cycle theories, of course, differs among writers. For example, Haberler (1963) classifies cycle theories as pure monetary, overinvestment, underconsumption, psychological, and other exogenous theories. Schumpeter (1954) classifies them simply as monetary and nonmonetary theories. Haberler's classification is a bit more sophisticated than Schumpeter's, because it takes into account the distinction between exogenous and endogenous theories, as well as the distinction between monetary and nonmonetary theories.

18

second contains a review of interwar business cycle theories. The last and main section discusses the treatment of equilibrium price theory in interwar business cycle theories.

Theories of crisis in the nineteenth century

Underconsumption theory

Even though the eighteenth century had witnessed the commercial crisis of 1763, 1772, 1783, and 1793, its writers did not develop any systematic ideas about the underlying causes of crises. It was only amidst the violent fluctuations in trade following the Napoleonic Wars that serious discussions of business crises began.

Malthus, in an attempt to explain the post-Napoleonic depression, developed an underconsumption theory of crisis. He observed that, after the war, the cessation of war expenditures, the reduction of taxes, and the consequent increase in saving caused a contraction of the "effectual" or effective demand compared with existing capital (Malthus, 1836, esp. pp. 418–19). That is, there was an underconsumption of commodities in the postwar period. The consequence of this glut would be a fall in prices and profits, which would undermine the country's wealth:

Commodities would be everywhere cheap. Capital would be seeking employment, but would not easily find it; and the profits of stock would be low. There would be no pressing and immediate demand for capital, because there would be no pressing and immediate demand for commodities. (Malthus, 1836, p. 415)

Furthermore, "under these circumstances, the saving from revenue to add to capital, instead of affording the remedy required, would only aggravate the distresses of the capitalists" (p. 415).[2] According to Malthus, a true solution to the problem at hand,and therefore the fundamental cause of crises, lay in the distribution of wealth. Given that capitalists' and landlords' propensity to consume was much weaker than that of workers, a more equitable distribution of wealth would help to increase the effective demand. However, Malthus opposed the idea of equal distribution on

In fact, classifications in the literature usually follow the criteria distinguishing either between monetary and nonmonetary theories or between exogenous and endogenous theories, or both. In this chapter, Haberler's classification is adopted.

[2] This recognition of oversaving as a source of stagnation makes Malthus's theory an underconsumption theory of the oversaving type in Schumpeter's classification scheme. Schumpeter distinguishes three types of underconsumption theories, namely, the oversaving type, the nonspending type that "emphasizes disturbances which arise from saving decisions that are *not* offset by decisions to invest," and the mass-poverty type that "attributes gluts to the inability of labor, owing to low wages, to 'buy its own product.'" See Schumpeter (1954, p. 740n).

broad grounds of social philosophy (pp. 426–7). Instead, he suggested unproductive expenditure by capitalists and landlords. "The employment of the poor in the roads and public works, and a tendency among landlords and persons of property to build, to improve and beautify their grounds, and to employ workmen and menial servants, are the means most within our power and most directly calculated to remedy the evils arising from that disturbance in the balance of produce and consumption" (p. 430).

In many respects, Malthus's idea is obscure;[3] however, his oversaving argument could be modestly interpreted in modern terms as follows. There exists an optimal proportion between consumption and saving that guarantees optimal or maximal growth of the economy. But the existing system of distribution or the satiability of consumer tastes in the short run prevents the maintenance of this optimal proportion, leading to a general glut.[4] In other words, capital accumulation in a growing economy inevitably accompanies the tendency to oversave, and this disturbs the optimal proportion between consumption and saving. As soon as markets are glutted, prices fall, profits fall, and the slump is on.

Sismondi, observing the English depressions of the postwar period, also suggested an underconsumption theory of crises in his *Nouveaux principes d'économie politique*, published in 1819. According to Sismondi, business crises are caused by the inherent complexity and planlessness of the capitalist economy.[5] More precisely, four factors are responsible for crises. The first is the planlessness of capitalist production and business organiza-

[3] Since Keynes (1951) expressed his somewhat exaggerated praise of Malthus as his true intellectual ancestor, there have been controversies over the correctness of Malthus's analysis of the general glut and the relation between Keynes and Malthus. For instance, Blaug (1985) takes Malthus to task for the flaws in his argument, saying that "it is fortunate for the history of economics that good logic triumphed over bad. A victory for Malthus would have made economics the happy hunting-ground of every quack ready with panaceas to cure the allegedly inherent defects of the market economy" (p. 175). Regardless of the soundness of Blaug's charge, it would be at least true that Malthus's writings are unclear and leave room for misunderstanding. For the general glut controversy, see the bibliographies in Rashid (1977) and Blaug (1985, pp. 176–8).

[4] For the satiability of consumer tastes in Malthus's model of general gluts, see Rashid (1977).

[5] See Mitchell (1927, pp. 4–7). Sismondi has been praised by many Marxist economists as an originator of underconsumption cycle theory, which plays an important part in Marxist critiques of the capitalist economy. Though Marxist theory of the cycle itself would be an interesting topic, in this book discussions about the Marxist tradition of cycle theory are limited to the cases in which that theory is closely related to classical tradition. For a historical investigation of Marxist cycle theories, see Bleaney (1976).

tion. The only guide a producer has in planning how much to produce is prices. But these prices do not carry sufficient information for correctly deciding the output in the near future. For example, the producer lacks knowledge of how his competitors and buyers will behave in the future in response to his production decisions. This idea resembles that of price misperception, which can be found both in the interwar cycle literature and in the more recent equilibrium business cycle theory. The second factor is overproduction. The purchasing power available for present output is the aggregate income of the previous year. Thus, if production continues to increase rapidly through the introduction of new technology, the gap between past income and present output will widen, and markets will come to be glutted. The third factor is oversaving, which is similar to the argument of Malthus. Finally, like Malthus, Sismondi argues that the fundamental cause of crises is the unequal distribution of wealth.

Unlike Malthus and Sismondi, the orthodox economists, such as Ricardo, Say, James Mill, and J. S. Mill, hold the view that a general glut is in principle impossible. Say's law of markets means that production cannot outrun demand, since demand depends on purchasing power, which in turn depends on production. Therefore, depressions are at most transitory phenomena during which an economy moves from one equilibrium to another and production is redirected toward more profitable areas. The postwar depressions were an instance of such a transition period:

The commencement of war after a long peace, or of peace after a long war, generally produces considerable distress in trade. It changes in a great degree the nature of the employments to which the respective capitals of countries were before devoted; and during the interval while they are settling in the situations which new circumstances have made the most beneficial, much fixed capital is unemployed, perhaps wholly lost, and labourers are without full employment. (Ricardo, 1951, p. 265).

Ricardo seemed to understand depressions as transitory phenomena but stopped there without pursuing the analysis of the adjustment to a new equilibrium. J. S. Mill presented a slightly more elaborate analysis. He understood that increased capital accumulation due to oversaving would result in a fall in interest rates and a rise in wages, along with a fall in prices as a consequence of an increased output of final goods. But Mill did not pay much attention to these consequences of increased capital accumulation in connection with business crises per se; rather, he thought that "the principle function of crises is to ward off the stationary state by the waste of capital and the unproductive consumptions which they bring" (Hutchinson, 1953, p. 353). In other words, Mill perceived crises as instances or phases of a long-run movement toward the stationary state. His main concern remained the theoretical exploitation of the normal course toward the stationary state and thus paid only secondary attention to the problem of crises.

Such an attitude was in fact common among classical economists in the nineteenth century:

The classical masters have paid but incidental attention to the rhythmical oscillations of trade in their systematic treatises. They have been concerned primarily to elucidate principles which hold "in the long run," or apply to the "normal state." (Mitchell, 1927, pp. 3–4)

Consequently, the study of crises took place outside the English classical tradition and was carried on mainly by critics of orthodox economics throughout the century. Moreover, the classical economists' denial of business crises as an economic problem might have been partially responsible for the prevalence of exogenous explanations of cycles in the latter half of the century, since the exogenous theory placed the main cause of crisis outside the economic system and thus was consistent with the classical conclusion that crises cannot be caused by inherent contradictions in the market system.

It is doubtless true that Keynes (1951) said the following while keeping his own economic theory in mind: "If only Malthus, instead of Ricardo, had been the present stem from which nineteenth-century economics proceeded, what a much wiser and richer place the world would be today!" (p. 120). However, the same might be said for the development of business cycle theory.

Exogenous theories of cycles

The glut controversy in the first half of the nineteenth century was the first serious discussion of the phenomena of depressions in the history of business cycle theory. However, classical writers in that period did not explicitly realize that crises and gluts were instances or phases of a longer process – the cycle. It was toward the turn of the century that the phenomena to be explained changed from crises to cycles. The most distinguished work in this context was Juglar's *Des crises commerciales et de leur retour periodique*, first published in 1860.

Juglar, first of all, developed a method of business cycle analysis that was succeeded by those of Tugan-Baranovsky, Mitchell, and, to some extent, Persons. To describe the phenomena more exactly and systematically, he used such time series data as prices, interest rates, and central bank balances and then proceeded to analyze the data in terms of phases and periodicity (see Schumpeter, 1954, p. 1124). (He himself found the periodicity to be roughly ten years.) By analyzing the data in this way, he found that the fundamental nature of crises lies in the successive phases of a recurring movement. Thus, the problem is not one of crises but one of cycles. That is, the causes of depression cannot be different from the causes of prosperity, and both depression and prosperity are caused by the same fundamental forces working within the economic system. In his own words, "The only cause of depression is prosperity" (quoted by Schumpeter, 1954, p. 1124).

Along with some progress toward a statistical description of the cycle phenomenon, as exemplified by the work of Juglar, the period under survey might be characterized as one of exogenous explanations of business cycles. John Mills elaborated a psychological explanation of cycles in his essay "On Credit Cycles and the Origin of Commercial Panics," published in 1867. Mills was not the first to notice the importance of psychological factors in the course of cycles. For example, J. S. Mill (1909) placed strong emphasis on external accidental factors that initiate profit expectations. Errors or irrationalities of optimism and pessimism are conceived as playing a role in the intensification of the rise and fall of business conditions. Mill, however, emphasizes that these psychological factors are almost accidental and not predictable.

In contrast, Mills emphasizes a definite, continuing rhythm in the psychology of businessmen.[6] He divides the credit cycle into four phases: collapse, depression, activity, and excitement, or panic, postpanic, recoil, and speculative periods. He then admits that the credit cycle describes the essential characteristic of commercial crises. But according to Mills, the conclusion that a want of currency is the fundamental cause of business cycles is that of "the jocular diagnosis that a man died of want of breath" (cited in Jones, 1900, p. 4). Development of credit can be traced to a parallel change of mood. "The malady of commercial crisis is not, in essence, a matter of *purse* but of the *mind*" (cited in Hansen, 1951, p. 269). More specifically, panic is the destruction of beliefs. The postpanic period is characterized by a slow recovery of confidence. Then comes the revival period, which is healthiest. During this period, commercial trade and manufacture are profitable, and people slowly begin to forget past panics. They assume that today's favorable business environment will be maintained in the future. This optimism, in turn, leads from healthy growth to credit excess and dangerous inflation. In this way, the recoil period changes into the speculation period. This pattern of alterations in the mental mood of businessmen appears to recur, with varying strength, throughout the course of the business cycle.

Another exogenous explanation was the famous sun-spot theory of Jevons (1884). Investigating the records of English trade from 1721 to

[6] The psychological theory of Mills is well described in Hansen (1951).

1878, Jevons found sixteen crises with an average interval of 10.466 years, which corresponded almost exactly to the periodicity of the sun-spot cycles – 10.45 years. The underlying idea was that if the periodicity of sun spots could be shown to have a counterpart in the fluctuation of harvests and if this fluctuation of harvests caused price fluctuations, then a causal link between sun spots and the periodicity of crises would be established. Citing a physical theory that sun spots were caused by the radiation of solar heat, Jevons explained the causal link between sun spots and harvests. That is, if their appearance was cyclical, there would be a consequent cyclical pattern in the amount of heat received by the earth. Furthermore, the amount of heat received would influence weather conditions, and differing conditions would create fluctuations in crops. The last casual connection in Jevons' chain, sun spots–heat–weather–crops–crises, was based on the credit theory of crisis. Noting the fact that the crises of 1836, 1839, 1847, and 1857 occurred in October and November, Jevons held that, during these months of harvest, a large amount of money was usually withdrawn to pay for harvest labor and other expenses. Therefore, in addition to this demand for money, if there was an unusually large demand for currency owing to a rise in the price of food caused by a bad harvest, a breakdown of the credit system might occur in the period of harvest.

It might be said that Jevons's theory depends too heavily on the theory of sun spots and meteorology to be a reliable theory of crisis. However, his idea of linking business cycles to a simple cyclical variation of natural phenomena that lies outside the economic system was so fascinating that many later speculative economists such as H. S. Jevons and H. L. Moore concerned themselves with the same idea.

Finally, to some economists like Roscher, a crisis was an abnormal event produced by outside disturbances. For example, Roscher argued that the more highly developed an economic system, the more difficult it was to maintain the market equilibrium, so that any factor that suddenly affected production or consumption could cause trouble. This argument is basically the same as Sismondi's analysis, according to which the fundamental cause of crisis is the complexity and planlessness of the capitalist economy, but Roscher's theory goes even farther in allowing the conclusion that each crisis has a unique external cause.[7] Business cycles are produced when the economic system is successively hit by exogenous disturbances such as the introduction of revolutionary inventions, the development of new transportation lines, wars, the return of peace, tariff revisions, monetary changes, crop failures, and changes in fashion (Mitchell, 1927).

---

[7] This conclusion can be identified as the position of the historical approach to business cycles. See Gordon (1949) for a discussion of this approach.

Interwar theories of business cycles

After about the turn of the century, business cycle research began to change.[8] First it was the cycle as a whole and the interconnection between its phases, rather than a single crisis, that was the main concern of study. Writings on the cycle tended to contain discussions of how the economy passed through different phases of the cycle, and reflecting this tendency the term "business cycles" or "trade cycles" came to be preferred to "commercial crises."

There was also an increasing tendency to treat the cycle not as a consequence of exogenous disturbances, but as an endogenous consequence of capitalistic development. Endogenous explanations of cycles as normal processes of the capitalist economy became so popular, at least among cycle theorists, that strictly exogenous explanations of cycles as abnormal consequences of outside disturbances of the equilibrium process, although consistent with the classical tradition, seemed to be of little appeal. The prevalence of endogenous explanations might reflect the fact that business cycle research had become a substantially independent subject of study, but at the same time it reflects the growing gap felt by most cycle theorists between business cycle theories and classical economics. Cycle theorists "were either highly critical of the equilibrium analysis of 'normal' value, price and distribution, or, if they accepted this analysis, found little or no application for its concepts and procedure in studying the trade cycle" (Hutchinson, 1953, p. 344). In contrast, economists in the classical tradition tended to ignore more and more the phenomena of cycles, treating cycle research as a mere special branch of equilibrium price analysis.

Most important, however, the "disproportionate" production argument came to be accepted by most cycle theorists as a valid theoretical proposition. The argument was first developed by classical economists such as Ricardo, James Mill, and J. S. Mill in defense of Say's law of markets, or the impossibility of general glut. They suggested that crises are temporary phenomena during which the existing structure of production comes to be partly disproportionate with respect to demands for products, owing to exogenous disturbances. This basic argument was sustained throughout the nineteenth century in various cycle theories, such as those of undercon-

---

[8] The cycle theories discussed in this section are not exactly products of the interwar period (1919–39). Rather the survey covers the period from about 1890 to the late 1930s. However, emphasis is given to the interwar cycle theories that have some connection to the main topic of the chapter, the relation between equilibrium and the business cycle.

sumption, overinvestment, and capital shortage. In this tradition, the argument was a complement to the validity of the impossibility of general gluts. However, a group of Continental economists, more or less influenced by Marxist theory and firmly disapproving of Say's law, also adopted the disproportionate production argument as a basis of their business cycle theory. Tugan-Baranovsky, Spiethoff, and Aftalion were among those who adopted this line of thinking. The argument came to be a main theme of nonmonetary business cycle theories in the twentieth century.[9]

Nonmonetary theories of cycles

In Germany and France, business cycle theory was highly respected during the second half of the nineteenth century, during which time cycle theory in England remained unorthodox and rudimentary. Say's law was under steady criticism, and underconsumption doctrines were well supported on the Continent. Rodbertus's underconsumption analysis was influential, and some elements of Marx's theory also reinforced the status of business cycle research on the Continent.

During the period under survey, from about 1900 to the late 1930s, nonmonetary cycle theories were developed mostly in Germany, where, according to Hayek, monetary explanations of cycles were largely mistrusted (see Hayek, 1933, esp. p. 30). Tugan-Baranovsky's and Spiethoff's theories are representative of such Continental cycle theories. Another group of nonmonetary cycle theories includes that of Aftalion, which received a great deal of support and was elaborated during the interwar period. According to Haberler's classification, the former group of theories, that represented by the work of Tugan-Baranovsky and Spiethoff, can be considered vertical maladjustment theory. The work of Aftalion corresponds to horizontal maladjustment theory.[10] A last group of theories,

---

[9] Schumpeter, in this respect, argues that the common ground for cycle theories during the interwar period was the "expansion of plant and equipment." That is, most theories start from such concepts as capital good industries and investment and saving, which are properties derived from characteristics of the physical process of capitalist production. Thus, to Schumpeter (1954) "most theories of cycles are nothing but different branches of that common trunk, 'plant and equipment'" (p. 1128). See also ibid., pp. 1125–32. Roughly speaking, however, Schumpeter's common ground, the expansion of plant and equipment, would be identical with the disproportionate production argument or with Haberler's "maladjustment in production."

[10] If the structure of production does not correspond to "the decisions of the population as to spending and saving," it is vertical maladjustment. If the

though not nonmonetary in a strict sense, covers a variety of psychological and technological explanations.

The first group seeks the fundamental cause of cyclical fluctuations in fluctuations in the production of capital goods. Tugan-Baranovsky holds that the chaotic character of capitalist production, combined with its ruthless drive to accumulate capital, creates a tendency toward the overproduction of capital goods, that is, a disproportionate production of capital with respect to the loanable fund.[11]

The loanable fund, which is accumulated out of profit during a boom and out of savings from fixed incomes (e.g., salary, rent, interest) during a slump, grows at a fairly constant pace. During a slump, uninvested loanable funds are accumulated, for few businessmen wish to borrow. But as uninvested capital is accumulated and interest rates fall to a certain level, funds will begin to flow into investment, bringing prosperity. When loanable funds are nearly exhausted, interest rates rise to prohibitive levels, an overproduction of capital goods results, and consequently a crisis follows.[12] The reason for the failure of fixed capital to grow in the right proportion lies in the unequal distribution of income between capitalists and workers. "It is the inadequate renumeration of labor . . . which is the fundamental cause of the rapid accumulation of social capital, which in its turn provokes crises" (Tugan-Baranovsky, 1913, p. 279; quoted by Mitchell, 1927, p. 24).

Tugan-Baranovsky's explanation of the upper turning point is very similar to Malthus's oversaving theory, but an important difference is that, whereas Malthus does not clearly recognize a discrepancy between savings and investment,[13] Tugan-Baranovsky's analysis depicts the mechanism that links savings to investment.

---

structure of production does not correspond to "the decisions of consumers as to expenditure between various lines of consumption goods" or "the decisions of producers at every stage as to the distribution of their cost expenditure between different forms of input," it is horizontal maladjustment (Haberler 1963, p. 30).

[11] Here one can observe a Marxian influence. Tugan-Branovsky's logic of arriving at the overproduction of capital goods seems to duplicate Marx's logic behind the law of the tendency of falling profit rates.

[12] Tugan-Baranovsky compares the working of loanable fund to a steam engine. When the pressure of the steam against the piston reaches some level, the piston is set in motion and is pushed to the end of the cylinder. Then the steam escapes and the piston returns to its initial position. The accumulation of loanable funds is analogous to the role of the steam in the cylinder. The fund begins to be invested in fixed capital when its accumulation reaches a certain level. When exhausted, the economy returns to the initial position – crisis. See Hansen (1951, pp. 289–90).

[13] In fact, that Malthus failed to recognize the discrepancy between savings and

Spiethoff, elaborating Tugan-Baranovsky's somewhat rigid system, presents another picture of savings and investment.[14] He accepts Tugan-Baranovsky's view that the essential character of the industrial cycle can be found in the fluctuation of investment, not in consumption. Unlike his predecessor, however, Spiethoff emphasizes aspects of investment demand, geographical discoveries, and technological advances (Hansen, 1951). An upswing during recessions is initiated by a sudden increase in investment demand, which is created by special factors such as innovations and the opening of new overseas markets. Whatever the impulse, the important fact is that an upswing is initiated by an investment vacuum. Prosperity is nothing but the result of the filling of that vacuum. Then a period of overproduction arises, not only from the unequal distribution of income, but also from the impossibility of foreseeing the future in a capitalist economy and of judging the size of the investment vacuum. It might be said that Spiethoff describes the cycle in terms of investment demands, in contrast with Tugan-Baranovsky's emphasis on savings (loanable fund). Both understand the discrepancy, however, between savings and investment as a key feature of cycles.

The second group of cycle theories, which also finds the ultimate cause of cyclical fluctuations in disproportionate production is represented by Aftalion's acceleration theory. His main thesis is that "the chief responsibility for cyclical fluctuation should be assigned to one of the characteristics of modern industrial technique, namely, the long period required for the production of fixed capital" (Aftalion, 1927, p. 165). Owing to the long duration of the capitalist process of production, the producer faces the difficulty of adjusting the stock of fixed capital to the final demand (a

investment is an important difference between Malthus and Keynes. When this is fully appreciated, Keynes's interpretation of Malthus as a true forerunner of his theory of effective demand becomes less convincing. See Bleaney (1976).

[14] Along with Tugan-Baranovsky and Spiethoff, Robertson notes the importance of the discrepancy between savings and investment in explaining cyclical fluctuations. However, his theory emphasizes the independent role of the banking system, which links savings to investment. The banking system can fill capital shortages during a boom by expanding the currency and raising prices. But this inflationary process cannot be sustained indefinitely. Banks raise interest rates and limit money loans. Eventually, the actual shortage of capital cannot be overcome even by the coordinating power of the banking system. Robertson (1926) understands the cycle as being caused basically by real factors. At the same time he does not fail to take into account the monetary aspect. Because of this, his theory is sometimes classified as a constructive synthesis (Haberler, 1963; Hutchison, 1953), sometimes classified with caution as an overinvestment theory (Hansen, 1951; Mitchell, 1927).

vertical maladjustment of production). Furthermore, the durability of capital goods prolongs the periods of boom and depression. Under this circumstance, a small disturbance in the final demand entails wide fluctuations in the demand for durable capital goods (the acceleration principle.)

Put another way, the capitalist process of production forces the producer to forecast the prices he will obtain after the production period. His expectations of future prices, however, are based on today's prices, which reflect the present final demands. Furthermore, the producer "has paid out long before in money the various elements in his costs at the *earlier* rates (for his raw materials, labor, etc.), when the falling in his selling price occurs" (Aftalion, 1909, p. 116; quoted by Hutchinson, 1953, p. 389). In other words, "there is a long delay which often separates the moment when the production of goods is decided upon and a forecast is made from the moment when the manufacture is terminated, and the forecast is replaced by reality" (Aftalion, 1927, p. 165). Consequently, optimistic (or pessimistic) expectations formulated at the beginning of the process persist until the forecast must face the test of reality after the long period of roundabout production. This explains the rhythm in the expectations of businessmen that has been noticed by many cycle theorists. Once the initial expectations fail to be realized owing to later disturbances in the final demand, the process of accelerating the disturbances starts to work. In short, Aftalion's theory of cyclical fluctuations explains overproduction as the accelerated outcome of a change in the final demand, and its underlying cause is the capitalist roundabout method of production, which Böhm-Bawerk also claimed.[15]

Finally there is the third group of theories that view the cycle as a consequence of exogenous causes. Pigou's work belongs in this group, even though the broader scope of his argument should not be ignored.[16] Pigou's

---

[15] As discussed in Chapter 1, Kydland and Prescott (1982) have developed a business cycle model that is based on the multiperiod construction of capital goods and have demonstrated the serial correlation of output time series. However, their "time to build" assumption is simply the first implication of the roundabout method of production – it takes time to produce. Another important implication is the acceleration principle, which Kydland and Prescott do not consider in their model. It is somewhat odd that, even if advances in modeling techniques, and thus modeling difficulties, are taken into account, Aftalion's model of the 1910s is much richer in content than today's cycle models.

[16] Although Pigou's theory makes an important contribution to business cycle research, it is dealt with here only to the extent that it is relevant to the main topic of this chapter. For the same reason, important cycle theories such as those of Schumpeter, Clark, and Mitchell are not discussed.

cycle theory might be classified as employing an exogenous monetary and psychological type of explanation, elements of which can be found in the writings of J. S. Mill, John Mills, and Marshall. But more important, it was Pigou who brought the distinction between impulse and propagation mechanism into general use.[17] He classifies the causation of industrial fluctuations into impulses and conditions (Pigou, 1927, pp. 7–9). When impulses, such as autonomous monetary changes, real factors, and psychological factors, come into play, they operate on a certain complex of industrial and monetary conditions. "Given the impulse, these will determine the nature of the effect that it produces, and are in this sense, causes of industrial fluctuations" (Pigou, 1927, p. 8). In discussing causes, he explicitly distinguishes psychological factors from expectations.[18]

Expectations based on these [real causes] are true, or valid expectations. Psychological causes . . . are changes that occur in men's attitude of mind, so that, on a constant basis of fact, they do not form a constant judgement. In a stationary state, or, more accurately, a state of self-repeating movement, real causes of varying expectations could not, by definition, exist. (Pigou, 1927, p. 30)

It follows that psychological causes do play a role as impulses in the form of errors of optimism and errors of pessimism. These errors tend to grow and spread via propagation mechanisms (Pigou's condition) such as financial ties that generate among businessmen a certain kind of psychological interdependence, and businessmen's reliance on other businessmen's expectations to justify their own.

Pigou, then, postulates other causes and industrial and monetary conditions, giving relatively greater emphasis to psychological factors, general price levels, and harvest fluctuations. In this sense, his view of cycles is eclectic and does not neglect either real or monetary factors.

Monetary theories of cycles

Although most nonmonetary cycle theories were developed on the Continent, the monetary aspect of cyclical phenomena was not seriously studied there. In England, however, the importance of the monetary and credit

[17] In effect Wicksell (1935) was the first to call attention to the mechanism of impulse and propagation. Like Pigou (1927), Frisch (1933) recognized its importance for business cycle research. See Chapter 3.

[18] Collard (1983) claims that Pigou already understood the rational expectations hypothesis. Even if Collard's claim is granted, however, it is hardly true that Pigou held a systematic view of rational expectations. His concern was by and large restricted to the case of systematic errors of expectations – in his terms, psychological causes. In other words, he does not seem to have considered (rational) expectations to be an important factor in explaining industrial fluctuations.

process in the trade cycle was well recognized.[19] J. S. Mill understood that crises were in most cases accompanied by severe credit disturbances. James Mill did not distinguish general crises from credit fluctuations when he attempted to explain cyclical fluctuations simply by postulating a direct causal link between credit fluctuations and the rhythm of optimism and pessimism. Tooke went farther, suggesting the mechanism through which the monetary or credit movement influenced price and output movements.

However, it was also in the British tradition that the monetary aspect of cyclical fluctuations or the monetary theory in general characteristically failed to be absorbed into the orthodox classical theory – the theory of value, relative prices, and distribution. Although serious discussion of money and banking systems might be found in nineteenth-century writings, they are more or less descriptive and not systematic. A typical view of money was, as Mill (1909) said, that it "only exerts a distinct and independent influence of its own when it gets out of order" (p. 499).[20] Monetary theory remained largely outside the sphere of orthodox economics.

Coming into the twentieth century, the cleavage between classical theory and the monetary aspect of cycle phenomena became more and more clear. Both the reinforcement of classical doctrine by the Walrasian general equilibrium theory and the flowering of business cycle research early in the century ultimately led to the recognition of their fundamental differences. Economists in the classical tradition thought this cleavage could be bridged by the development of a satisfactory monetary theory, whereas business cycle theorists tended to deemphasize or ignore the body of classical theory, looking beyond equilibrium theory for other schemes.

Both sides, however, seemed to agree on the complexity of the phenomena to be explained. Because of this complexity, no theory contained a simple explanation of the cycle. Most theories did not ignore either real or monetary factors, but their emphasis differed. An exception was the work of Hawtrey. Hawtrey (1923) held an extreme monetary position, claiming that "the trade cycle is a purely monetary phenomenon" (p. 141).[21] He

---

[19] There were also a few monetary writings by Continental cycle theorists like Juglar and Wagner, but their influence was limited. In the Continental tradition, nonmonetary theories dominated the study of business cycles, and cycle theorists gave little attention to monetary aspects of business cycles. This might partly reflect the fact that throughout the nineteenth century the banking and credit system in Continental countries was less developed than it was in England.

[20] Neil de Marchi at Duke University noted this beautiful quote in a private conversation, for which the author is grateful.

[21] Fisher (1925) also concluded that changes in price level or the purchasing power of money almost completely explain fluctuations in trade. It is interesting,

found a fundamental cause of the cycle to be the inherent instability of credit or the failure of the banking system to adjust the real rate of interest when the value of money is changing.

Adopting the income approach to the theory of money and prices, the seed of which can be found in Tooke (see Marget, 1938), Hawtrey analyzed the influence of money on the real economy in the following way. When new money is created, the public holds an undue proportion of cash balances with respect to their income; thus, they tend to spend more. Traders consequently find that increased consumer outlays have reduced their stocks of goods below a desirable level, and thus order more goods to rebuild the stocks. Moreover, since sales have increased, they want a level of stocks that is higher than the previous level. This requires more borrowing and a further extension of bank credit.

But bank credit is not unlimited. It is something like a reservoir (Hawtrey, 1947). When banking authorities realize that the level of bank reserves is too low, they begin to contract credit by adjusting interest rates. Consequently, consumer outlays are curtailed, traders' stocks of goods accumulate, and there is a contraction of bank credit. Then banking authorities find that they have an unusually high level of bank reserves and create new money by lowering interest rates.

In this setting, the reason for the drain (overflow) of bank reserves during a credit expansion (contraction) – thus the reason for the regular recurrence of expansion and contraction of credit – lies in the slow response of people's cash holdings to credit movements. When credit is expanded, it does not immediately increase people's income and cash holdings. This process takes considerable time. Cash holdings lag behind income, and income in turn lags behind credit movement (a kind of rigidity of wage rates). Thus, while an increasing amount will be retained in the public's cash holdings, there will be a drain on cash out of the holdings of the banks, eventually creating a drain on reserves. Given the lagged response of people's cash holdings to credit movement, "so long as credit is regulated with reference to reserve propositions, the trade cycle is bound to recur" (Hawtrey, 1923, p. 144).

Hawtrey's extreme monetary explanation of the cycle cannot escape the charge of oversimplification. Completely ignoring the importance of non-monetary factors, Hawtrey (1913) concludes that "whereas the influences

however, that he doubted the existence of business cycles, suggesting that the cycle we observe merely comprises fluctuations above and below the economy's average trend. That is to say, the economy fluctuates around its mean just as luck at Monte Carlo does. For more recent elaborations of Fisher's "Monte Carlo cycle" that negate the very existence of cycles, see McCulloch (1975) and Anderson (1977).

arising out of the banking system are very important, those which arise from the conditions of production and consumption have but little bearing (except perhaps in the case of actual famine) upon the state of trade as a whole" (p. 130). Furthermore, Hawtrey contends that a change in the rate of interest, caused by the banking authorities' credit policy, affects the economic system, not through a direct influence on investment in fixed capital, but through the provision of working capital and particularly stocks of goods (see Haberler, 1963). Hence, the real economy maintains a relatively stable equilibrium state, but under the monetary economy this real equilibrium becomes vulnerable to the fluctuations of credit to the extent that movements of interest rates disturb the stability of working capital and stocks of goods.

Although oversimplified, Hawtrey's propositions can be found in the theories of many later writers. Monetarists (see Friedman and Schwartz, 1963a, b), New Classical economists, and to some extent Hayek have accepted Hawtrey's propositions that the inherent instability of credit is an important cause and aspect of the cycle, that there would be no cyclical fluctuations in a barter economy, and that the fundamental cause of the cycle therefore lies in the movement of the money supply.

Hayek's theory of monetary overinvestment

Hawtrey's monetary explanation of business cycles presents a picture in which monetary movements influence the economic system through changes in interest rates; however, the influence is confined to working capital, and the effect of the change in interest rates on investment in fixed capital is considered unimportant. To Hawtrey, the deep structure of production is largely independent of the influence of monetary movement, and business cycles are purely monetary phenomena that do not affect the deep structure.

In contrast, Hayek (1933) examines primarily the mechanism through which monetary factors influence the real structure of production: "While I have . . . emphasized the *monetary causes* which *start* the cyclical fluctuations, I have . . . concentrated on the *successive changes in the real structure of production*, which constitute those fluctuations" (p. 17; emphasis in the original). Monetary factors cause the cycle, but real phenomena constitute the cycle. In the terminology of Frisch (1933), Hayek's thesis might be understood as employing the monetary impulse and the real propagation mechanism.[22]

---

[22] On the other hand, Hawtrey's monetary explanation might be recast in terms of the monetary impulse and the monetary propagation mechanism. As Frisch (1933) said, "Knut Wicksell seems to be the first who has been definitely aware

Hayek adopts ideas of Wicksell as a starting point in his theory of business cycles.[23] Wicksell (1936) showed how the Böhm-Bawerkian or natural rate of interest could diverge from the money rate of interest. Banks could initiate a cumulative process away from equilibrium by creating money, thus lowering the market rate of interest below the natural rate that would equate real investment with voluntary saving. Hayek extends this cumulative process by focusing on the roundaboutness of capitalist production.

A lowering of the market rate will lead to a lengthening of the period of production. That is, a lowering of the market rate will raise the proportion of entrepreneurs' expenditures on producers' goods to the expenditure on consumption goods; prices of producers' goods will go up and their production will increase relative to that of consumers' goods. Then an investment-induced boom will take place. However, the ratio of consumer demand to investment demand is different from that of income allocated between saving and consumption, since the adjustment of wages to the increase in money is slow (Hayek, 1932). "Yet as soon as the competition of entrepreneurs for the factors of production has driven up wages in proportion to the increase in money, and no additional credits are forthcoming, the proportion which they are able to spend on capital goods must fall" (Hayek, 1932, p. 243). This means that, since the income allocation between saving and consumption has returned to around the previous equilibrium state, the new roundaboutness of production turns out to be too lengthy compared with the increased consumption demand. A

of the two types of problems in economic cycle analysis – the propagation problem and the impulse problem – and also the first who has formulated explicitly the theory that the sources of energy which maintain the economic cycles are erratic shocks. . . . He illustrates it by one of those perfectly simple and yet profound illustrations; 'If you hit a wooden rocking-horse with a club, the movement of the horse will be very different from that of the club' " (p. 198). Even if the influence of Wicksell is granted, it is interesting that, in spite of the dearth of communication between quantitative cycle researchers like Frisch and Slutsky and descriptive cycle theorists like Hayek, Pigou, and Aftalion, both groups have almost simultaneously come up with essentially the same idea about cyclical fluctuations. This might be another small example of simultaneous discovery in the history of economics that suggests the possibility of rationally reconstructing the history of economics – the internal history. For discussions about the internal history, see Lakatos and Musgrave (1970), Latsis (1976), and Weintraub (1985).

[23] Keynes in his *Treatise* also gave credit to Wicksell. However, "what was in common between [Keynes and Hayek] – all that seemed to be in common between them – was the intellectual descent which each claimed from Wicksell; but Wicksell plus Keynes said one thing, Wicksell plus Hayek said quite another" (Hicks, 1967, p. 204).

crisis then takes place, resulting in an excess capacity for producing durable capital goods and consequently unemployment. Thus, it might be said that Hayek's theory is the exposition of the cyclical sequence of induced lengthening and reshortening of the capitalist production process, based on an analysis of the price mechanism (see Machlup, 1976).

As is well known, Hayek's theory of business cycles builds on an Austrian tradition. His rejection of the quantity theory of money can be directly traced to Mises's theory of money, and the explanation of the cyclical sequence in terms of relative prices is strictly in line with the Austrian emphasis on equilibrating processes of individuals. As Machlup (1976) notes, Hayek demonstrates that

almost any change in the quantity of money influences relative prices, no matter whether or not it changes the general price level; and that the real task of the theory of money is to show the influences of changes in quantity and distribution of money upon the exchange ratios between different goods and upon the allocation of resources to the production of different goods.

Considering the effect of the change in the quantity of money on the price level as secondary in importance, Hayek describes, in explaining the lengthening of the period of production, how individual entrepreneurs reallocate their factors of production in accordance with relative factor prices and how individual consumers react to the change in the quantity of money by allocating income between saving and consumption. Individuals' rational behaviors, however, have to confront misdirected production and crisis, since the price signals sent by the monetary system are misleading. In Hayek's (1933) words, "In the exchange economy, production is governed by prices, independently of any knowledge of the whole process on the part of individual producers, so that it is only when the pricing process is itself disturbed that a misdirection of production can occur" (pp. 85-5). In this sense, cyclical fluctuations are nothing but an inevitable consequence of the individual's misled equilibrating process, caused by a monetary disturbance and by the individual's limited ability to observe such monetary aggregates accurately.

Under Hayek's scheme, the business cycle policy should stress the establishment of a stable money supply that keeps money neutral.[24] "If it were possible . . . to keep the total amount of bank deposits entirely stable, that would constitute the only means of getting rid of cyclical fluctuations." But this aspiration is purely utopian, for the "stability of the economic system would be obtained at the price of curbing economic progress" (Hayek, 1933, pp.190-1). In other words, a constant quantity of money in

[24] According to Hayek, money is neutral if all relative prices among goods and services are what they would be if money did not exist, as in a barter economy. See Hayek (1935, pp. 129-31).

a growing economy cannot satisfy conditions of neutral money. Furthermore, even in a stationary economy neutral money is attainable only if the money supply is constant, if all prices are completely flexible, and if all contracts are based on a correct anticipation of future price movement (Hayek, 1935). Therefore, it cannot be a goal of monetary policy to keep money neutral, and "the utmost that can be achieved . . . is only a mitigation, never the abolition of the Trade Cycle" (Hayek, 1933, p. 192). These discussions of an ideal money system, however, provide the theoretical basis for Hayek's opposition to an elastic system in which monetary authorities try to manage the quantity of money so as to keep the value of money stable. To Hayek, management of the quantity of money is just another disturbance, and an elastic system of controlling cyclical fluctuations even has the potential to amplify fluctuations rather than mitigate them.

Hayek's theory of industrial fluctuations, however, did not succeed in persuading English economists in the 1930s. Most reviews of his book *Prices and Production*, which was published in 1931, were not favorable. Rather than trying to understand some of Hayek's central ideas, the reviewers seemed to jump directly into criticism of his theoretical propositions and policy conclusions.[25]

Sraffa (1932), seeking to find logical inconsistencies in Hayek's theory, attacks Hayek fiercely. The focus is on Hayek's monetary theory and the Wicksellian theory of the natural rate of interest. Sraffa criticizes Hayek for ignoring the effect of changes in the general price level on production and neglecting such important functions of money as store of value and unit of account. According to Sraffa, Hayek's monetary theory is so "neutralized" that it cannot successfully show the fundamental differences between the monetary and nonmonetary economy, which is supposed to be the very starting point of Hayek's inquiry into business cycles. Therefore, Sraffa claims, when the quantity of money is changed, it could not have such consequences as lengthening or shortening the period of production, "since money has been thoroughly 'neutralized' from the start" so as not to include the effect of change of the general price level and other characteris-

---

[25] There was a strong Keynesian influence behind most criticisms of Hayek's theory. As is evident in his accusation of Hayek as a "wild duck" in the *General Theory*, Keynes almost always dismissed Hayek's important theoretical arguments, in particular the "forced savings" doctrine. It seems that Keynes's critical attitude toward Hayek is somehow adhered to by disciples like Sraffa, Harrod, and Kaldor. Therefore, their severe criticism of Hayek should be understood in the light of the fact that at the same time they are criticizing Hayek they are following and defending Keynes.

tics of money (Sraffa, 1932, p. 49). Apparently relying on the Ricardian idea of the standard commodity, Sraffa then faults Hayek for his criticism of Wicksell's criterion of neutral money.[26]

Robertson (1934) appreciates Hayek's theory as a description of special kinds of cycles, a description that is applicable to some industrial fluctuations in the nineteenth and early twentieth centuries, especially the crisis of 1909. He does not, however, accept Hayek's cycle theory as a general theory of the business cycle.

Harrod (1934) dismisses Hayek's thesis that an infusion of new money would cause disturbances in the relative price system and thus in the structure of production, by demonstrating the possibility that in a growing economy, if new money is created at the same rate as income growth, then a stable price level will be maintained and there will be no disturbance in the relative price system.

Somewhat later, in 1942, Kaldor (1942) critically reviewed Hayek's new book, *Profits, Interest and Investment*, focusing on the "Ricardo effect."[27] The Ricardo effect "asserts that in conditions of full employment an increase in the demand for consumer goods will produce a decrease of investment, and vice versa" (Hayek, 1969, p. 274).[28] As the demand for consumer goods increases, the prices of consumer goods will increase and real wages will fall. Consequently, on one hand, there will be an increase in investment in order to meet the increased demand for consumer goods, and on the other hand, owing to the fall in real wages, less capitalistic methods of production will be adopted, so that investment in capital goods will be reduced. Hayek asserts that the second tendency overshadows the first, and a decline in investment will eventually result. Through his analysis of "profit margins" – the ratio between factor prices and product prices – Hayek (1935) describes how each entrepreneur aiming to maximize his profits chooses the combination of less capital and more labor in response to the increase in profit margins, that is, the fall in real wages. But Kaldor doubts the

[26] For Sraffa's reinterpretation of Ricardo and the standard commodity, see Sraffa (1960).

[27] Kaldor (1942) preferred the "Concertina effect" to the Ricardo effect, since he could not find in Ricardo's writing the effect that Hayek attributed to Ricardo. Schumpeter (1939), recognizing an original aspect of Hayek's theory, called it the "Hayek effect," but Hayek (1969) himself did not wish "what [he] regarded as an old-established doctrine to be regarded as an innovation" (p. 247n) and insisted on calling it the Ricardo effect. For an evaluation of Hayek's Ricardo effect, see Moss and Vaughn (1986).

[28] However, in *Profits, Interest and Investment*, Hayek argues that the Ricardo effect would hold even if there were unemployment and there were no change in money wages and interest rates.

validity of the Ricardo effect from the Keynesian viewpoint. Emphasizing the role of profits, he reaches a different conclusion, namely, that a rise in demand for consumer goods would lead to the possibility of higher profits and these would then induce an increase in investment demand. Furthermore, Kaldor (1942) is not certain that the factor substitutions between labor and capital in the short run are as flexible as Hayek assumes.[29]

One important aspect of these controversies over the Ricardo effect is its policy implication. If the Ricardo effect holds, it is directly implied that any trade cycle policy aiming to avoid crises should be one of keeping down consumption to a level that is compatible with the completion of already invested projects (Hayek, 1942). On the contrary, the Keynesian prescription is that of expanding expenditures such as consumer outlays and investment. As history later proved, Keynes's underinvestment theory was victorious over Hayek's theory of overinvestment. But this does not necessarily mean that Hayek's model is theoretically invalid. In particular, in the case of the Ricardo effect, one cannot be certain whether Keynes's argument, that an increase in demand for consumer goods leads to an increase in investment demand, would hold unambiguously even under full employment. Investment and consumption goods could be competitive under full employment. In the same way, Hayek's Ricardo effect might not occur in a situation of general unemployment. In that situation investment and consumption goods could be complementary.

Although it should be granted that, considering the tendency toward quantitive economics during the interwar period, Hayek's theory presented certain difficulties to one who might want to mathematize it, this does not fully explain why Hayek was ignored, though not rejected, by contemporary and later economists. Here Machlup could be right in noting that "with the appearance of the *General Theory* the drama was ended. By then, after several years of the Great Depression, it had become clear that Hayek's prescription of 'waiting it out' was inopportune" (Machlup, 1976, p. 26). Along with his unacceptable policy conclusion of "waiting it out" in the middle of the Depression, Hayek's introduction to English audiences of "the intolerably cumbersome theory of capital derived from Jevons and Böhm-Bawerk . . . [which is] a noteworthy new departure in the metaphysics of political economy . . . [but] is singularly ill-adapted for use in monetary theory" (Hawtrey, 1932, p. 125) might be another factor that contributed to the unfortunate fate of Hayek's theory. "The obstacle which confronted one on his side was his Böhm-Bawerkian model; an analytical framework that had become familiar, even orthodox, in some continental

---

[29] This controversy over the Ricardo effect parallels the recent controversy between monetarists and Keynesians over the spillover effect of fiscal policy.

countries, but was unfamiliar in England. *Prices and Production* was written in English, but it was not English economics. It needed further translation before it could be properly assessed" (Hicks, 1967, p. 204). However, a full translation was never attempted.

Equilibrium theory and interwar theories of cycles

Equilibrium and business cycles

As discussed in the preceding section, it was not until the interwar years that the question of the relation between business cycle theory and equilibrium theory came to be seriously addressed. Equilibrium theory in the interwar years was generally understood as a Walrasian theory of the interdependent system in that a set of equilibrium prices was deduced from given data, such as tastes and technologies. However, when the logic of equilibrium theory was applied to cycles, no satisfactory explanation of the phenomena could be derived.[30] Strictly interpreted, empirical observations of cyclical fluctuations should correspond to a continuum of equilibrium in which the economic system successively reacts to external disturbances by instantaneously forming a new equilibrium, but the phenomena of cycles more closely resemble a breakdown of the system of equilibrium than a continuum of equilibrium. To some cycle theorists like Mitchell, equilibrium theory seemed to be without empirical content and therefore useless, and to most economists cyclical fluctuations were at least strong empirical evidence for unsatisfactory lacunae in economic theory.

Confronted with such a cleavage between business cycle theory, on the one hand, and equilibrium theory, on the other, one could pursue three possible courses. The first would be to drop or revise some secondary assumptions and rather boldly attempt to build a cycle theory somehow based on such indispensable principles as rational economic behavior and the interdependence of activities. The second would be to elaborate and extend equilibrium price theory, not believing in the immediate possibility of explaining the business cycle by the existing body of equilibrium theory, but hoping that the expanded theory would eventually incorporate the phenomenon of the cycle. The last possibility would be simply to reject equilibrium theory, concentrating on empirical studies without the help of theory, until a plausible, empirically based new theoretical framework could be constructed. The approach of the National Bureau of Economic Research to business cycles is representative of this last possibility.

In a sense, it might be said that most interwar cycle theories fall into the first group. Pigou's psychological explanation of the cycle means that

[30] For a criticism of equilibrium theory from this point of view, see Kuznets (1930).

businessmen do not rationally form their expectations (an abandonment of rational economic behavior). In many cycle theories, the price mechanism of supply and demand instantaneously reaching equilibrium was revised so as to allow for lags in adjustment. And in the case of nonmonetary theories, additional assumptions like the roundaboutness of capitalist production were introduced.

As such most interwar cycle theories built a scheme more or less based on some propositions from equilibrium theory. In most cases, however, their revision of equilibrium theory or introduction of new assumptions was so crucial to their explanation of the cycle that the *indispensable principles* of equilibrium theory, such as the price mechanism and the notion of rationality, had to be regarded as being of secondary importance. The principles of equilibrium theory were not successfully applied to business cycles; in other words, the cycle could not be described in principle as a consequence of individuals' rational behaviors or the price mechanism.

Unlike those who adhered to the prevailing skepticism, particularly in England and Germany, as to the possibility of constructing an equilibrium theory of business cycles, Austrian economists did not doubt that the real world *should be* and *could be* understood as proceeding toward equilibrium.[31] The Böhm-Bawerkian theory of capital and interest showed clearly how the roundaboutness of capitalistic production, one of the important features of the cycle, could be explained in terms of relative prices (interest rates). Menger and Mises established a subjective theory in which the basic laws of economics were interpreted as an outcome of individuals' interdependent actions. The Austrian tradition thus seemed very much consistent with the Lausanne school's world of general equilibrium; both emphasized the interdependence of individual plans, adopted the rationality of human action as a valid proposition, and assumed methodological individualism as a basic principle of their economics. There was, however, one fundamental methodological difference between the two schools. The Austrians rejected the assumption of Walras's auctioneer, which makes it possible for Walrasian theory to concentrate exclusively on the analysis of the mutual consistency of individual plans and the individual's behavior in equilibrium. In the world of the Austrians, the fundamentals of capitalist society lay in the "equilibrating process," in that individual plans were carried out independently of the existence of equilibrium, and the state of equilibrium was eventually arrived at through this process. This theory of equilibrating process had important advantages over Walrasian theory. Whereas money could not be adequately introduced in the Walrasian framework, the denial

---

[31] For a brief introduction to the tradition of Austrian economics, see Hayek (1968).

of the assumption of a Walrasian auctioneer opened up for the Austrians the possibility of developing a theory of money and consequently of constructing cycle theories.

It was Hayek who actually built up a consistent Austrian theory of money and cycles. As the starting point of his inquiry, Hayek points out that "the difference between the course of events described by static [equilibrium] theory . . . and the actual course of events" is to be found in money. "Money being a commodity which, unlike all others, is incapable of finally satisfying demand, its introduction does away with the rigid interdependence and self-sufficiency of the 'closed' system of equilibrium" (Hayek, 1933, p. 44). Thus, the construction of a satisfactory theory of money is tantamount to forming the basis of a cycle theory. Hayek does this by further developing his concept of "neutral money." As for conditions of neutral money, he states:

It is quite conceivable that a distortion of relative prices and a misdirection of production by monetary influences could only be avoided if, *firstly,* the total money stream remained constant, and *secondly,* all prices were completely flexible, *and, thirdly,* all long term contracts were based on a correct anticipation of future price movements. (Hayek, 1935, p. 131)[32]

It follows from these conditions that cyclical fluctuations reflect the violation of all three conditions in a monetary economy. Therefore, business cycles are the consequence of monetary disturbances in the world of price rigidity and imperfect foresight. Expansions in the money supply tend to cause a divergence between the natural and market rates of interest, and entrepreneurs react to this artificial lowering of the market interest rate by choosing a more roundabout method of production, since their imperfect foresight prevents them from perceiving the correct relative prices between future goods and present goods. This error creates an investment boom. However, the wage response to expansions of the money supply is sluggish or rigid.[33] When wages do increase so as to reflect the influence of the monetary expansions fully (i.e., somewhat after the monetary expansion has come to an end), consumers' real income will also return to levels near the previous equilibrium levels and consumers will want to allocate their income between consumption and saving as they did before. But the

---

[32] Hayek's concept of neutral money is different from the modern sense of the neutrality of money. In today's analysis money can be said to be neutral if the second and third conditions above hold. Hayek's concept seems to indicate the state of the economy in which the monetary influence on the real economy is completely excluded *and* the value of money is constant.

[33] Here, if one assumes an instantaneous adjustment of wages, Hayek's theory is no longer a cycle theory. As Hicks (1967) correctly interprets it, Hayek's theory would in this case reduce to a growth theory.

entrepreneurs now produce less consumer goods because the method of production is more time consuming than it was before. At last the Ricardo effect starts to work, and a crisis is near.

This explanation should be understood at least as an attempt to construct a theory of cycles based on the principles of equilibrium theory – that is, rational economic behavior and the interdependence of individual activities – although the Austrian equilibrating process clearly substitutes for the Walrasian auctioneer.

Intertemporal equilibrium

Along with the endeavor to apply the principles of equilibrium theory to business cycles, there was an increasing awareness of the limitations of the equilibrium concept. Recognizing that conventional equilibrium theory was essentially static or timeless, most efforts were devoted to the introduction of the time element into the theory. One way of doing this was to relax the assumption of the instantaneous adjustment of the price mechanism, thereby directing attention toward a disequilibrium analysis.

Another way was to extend the concept of equilibrium to include time. In a paper published in 1928, Hayek (1984) developed the concept of intertemporal equilibrium. Individuals' planning horizons are assumed finite, and expectations during this period are perfect in the sense that the outcome of the resource allocation among individuals during the period is consistent with the decision made at the beginning of the period. In this case – perfect foresight within a period – the role of the price mechanism is basically the same as that in a static equilibrium system. "Prices . . . fulfil a particularly significant role with respect to the distribution of the individual processes through time, as the guide and regulator of all economic activity in the exchange economy" (Hayek, 1984, p. 71). The reason for the differences in the prices of technically equivalent goods at different points in time is that there exist difficulties or disutilities in transferring goods from one point in time to another, "in just the same way as such goods will not carry the same price if they are located at different places" (Hayek, 1984, p. 76).

This idea of a perfect foresight equilibrium within a period is extended by Hicks (1946, 1980). In Hicks's temporary equilibrium model, individuals make decisions on the basis of their expectations at the beginning of the "week," and then there is a temporary equilibrium through the week. At the end of the week, however, individuals realize that their expectations have not been fulfilled and revise their plan for the next week; as a result, another temporary equilibrium exists in the next week. For Hicks, a plausible picture of a dynamic system is thus a succession of such temporary equilibria. One might note that the idea of a planning horizon, or of intertemporal equilibrium within a period, is common to Hayek and Hicks.[34]

Hayek's notion of the intertemporal equilibrium is elaborated in his "Price Expectations, Monetary Disturbances and Malinvestments" (Hayek, 1944), first published in 1935. There, Hayek advances the idea of unfulfilled expectations due to misleading prices:

> It is probably clear . . . that expectations existing at a particular moment will to a large extent be based on prices existing at that moment and that we can conceive of constellations of such prices which will create expectations inevitably doomed to disappointment, and of other constellations which do not bear the germ of such disappointment and which will create expectations which – at least if there are no unforeseen changes in external circumstances – may be in harmony with the actual course of events. (p. 354)

It is possible, then, that if the price information can be misleading, all individuals "should . . . simultaneously make mistakes in the same direction" (Hayek, 1944, p. 354) since "the prices existing when they made their decisions and on which they had to base their views about the future have created expectations which must necessarily be disappointed (p. 353). When money is introduced into this picture as a source of price misperception, this becomes a theory of the cycle. "The cause of a crisis would be that entrepreneurs had mistakenly regarded a temporary increase in the supply of capital as permanent and acted in this expectation" (p. 356). In other words, when entrepreneurs are fooled by a temporarily increased money supply, a crisis occurs. Otherwise, the economy would run on in its normal course. The business cycle is therefore, to some degree, a consequence of misleading price information.[35]

Hayek's idea of the price mechanism as an information carrier is developed further in his later study of the market system, which shows that the efficiency of the capitalist economic system lies in the function of the market system as a network for utilizing information (see Hayek, 1937, 1945).

---

[34] The problem of a planning horizon – "the problem concerning the determination of the length of time which economic activity has in view" – does not seem to have been a familiar subject in England in the 1920s and 1930s (see Rosenstein-Rodan, 1934). This might confirm the Austrian influences, including Hayek's, on Hicks.

[35] One might notice the striking similarities between the ideas of Hayek and the recent equilibrium business cycle theory. This will be more discussed more fully in Chapter 4.

CHAPTER 3

The econometric approach to business cycles

This chapter is concerned mainly with the history of the econometric approach to business cycles. However, because the historical development of the approach is obviously associated with that of both business cycle theory and econometrics, the discussion must be broad enough to include the following issues, which could otherwise be dealt with separately.

The first issue is a fundamental methodological problem of econometrics. Given the fact that the data alone do not enable us to discover or reveal the laws governing them, it is obvious that *a priori* theory should play a role in the econometrician's search for truth. The extent to which economic theory should be introduced was a controversial issue in the earlier history of econometrics. *Theory without statistical inference, empirical investigations without theory,* and *econometrics as a bridge between theory and observations* are positions that could be roughly identified with such names as Keynes, Mitchell, and Koopmans, respectively. Even today, these positions can be found in various schools of econometrics. Later in the chapter, this issue will be discussed in the context of criticisms of the econometric approach to business cycles.

The second issue is related to the question of why and how the business cycle faded away as an independent subject of study. Starting in the late 1940s, the popularity of cycle theories began to decline, and they were eventually replaced by Keynesian macroeconomics. The usual explanation for this redirection of aggregate economics stresses both the advent of Keynesianism and historical experiences – for example, the fact that the postwar business cycle became mild and substantially stable (e.g., Bronfenbrenner, 1969). However, an important element of the truth concealed by the use of the single word "Keynesianism" is that Keynesianism is a product of Keynes's *General Theory* and the econometric movement combined.[1] An examination of the econometric movement, in particular the

---

[1] Lucas (1977, 1980) also points out that the Keynesian revolution was accompanied by the econometric movement and killed the interwar cycle theories. However, he deemphasizes the impact of the econometric movement, mainly accusing Keynes's theory of shifting aggregate economics from dynamic to static analysis.

44

development of the econometric approach to business cycles, would shed some light on the fate of the interwar cycle theories.

The econometric approach is, of course, a way of relating cycle theories to empirical data. One might think, therefore, that this approach itself is independent of theoretical developments in cycle research, since it can be seen basically as a matter of translating theoretical terms into empirical terms. But the situation is not so simple. As Weintraub (1986) demonstrated by showing that a conceptual change in the definition of equilibrium occurred in the course of the mathematical proof of the existence of general equilibrium, the quantification or mathematization of economic theory usually involves changes in its form and content. In the case of interwar cycle theories, the econometric approach forced economists to simplify their theories, to formulate them in terms of empirically measurable concepts, and to transform some key conceptions, which eventually led to the destruction of most arguments peculiar to interwar cycle theories. In this context, it is important to understand the historical process by which the econometric approach was established as a legitimate way of doing cycle research.

Econometrics followed two early courses of development: the measurement of demand curves and the analysis of business cycles. The first two sections of this chapter deal with these. It is interesting that both led to the recognition of simultaneous relationships between economic variables or of econometric structure. Yet it was the Cowles Commission that explicitly adopted the simultaneity idea, established the simultaneous-equation system estimation method, and advocated the econometric approach to business cycles. These are discussed in detail in the third section of this chapter. The last section discusses some important criticisms of the Cowles Commission method.

Demand analysis

The empirical demand curves of Moore and Schultz

It was not until the publication of H. L. Moore's work (1914) that economists began to pay serious attention to the problem of deriving empirical demand curves. Subsequently Schultz (1928, 1938) extended and elaborated Moore's method without making any major modifications, and throughout the 1920s and 1930s Moore and Schultz's method of measuring demand curves became more or less standard.

Their work is based on the theoretical demand analysis developed by the neoclassical school of Marshall, Cournot, and Walras. A profound obstacle to the straightforward measurement of demand curves was the static nature of the theoretical analysis, that is, the fundamental dependence of its validity on the assumption of *ceteris paribus*. The procedure Moore and Schultz developed to overcome this difficulty was essentially one of adjusting the data so as to eliminate the effect of time shifts from the economic data. It was hoped that the static law of demand could thereby be derived:

An ideal method would eliminate entirely all of the disturbing factors. We should then obtain perfect correlation between changes in the quantity demanded and corresponding changes in price. That is to say, the observations would all lie on the demand curve – there would be no "scatter" of points around the curve. (Schultz, 1928, p. 33)

The disturbing factors they recognized were "changes in the volume of the commodity that arise from the increasing population and changes in the level of prices which are the combined result of causes specifically responsible for price cycles and of causes that produce a secular trend in price" (H. L. Moore, 1914). The methods they developed to remove these factors were those of relative changes and trend ratios.

The method of relative changes involves adjusting the price and quantity data by taking the percentage of change in the value from one year to the next.[2] "By taking the relative change in the amount of the commodity that is demanded, instead of the absolute quantities, the effects of increasing population are approximately eliminated; and by taking the relative change in the corresponding prices instead of the corresponding absolute prices, the errors due to a fluctuating price level are partially removed" (H. L. Moore, 1914, p. 69).

The method of trend ratios eliminates the variations due to the influence of a secular trend from the price and quantity data, first by fitting a trend line to each time series and then by taking the ratios of the observed values to the fitted trend. The rationale for this method is as follows:

If, during the period when our observations were taken, "all other things" had remained equal as theory demands, we should have no secular trend either of prices or of quantities. The existence of a secular trend in either series is *prima facie* evidence that "all other things" did not remain equal, that there were one or more disturbing factors or elements. It is the "disturbing elements" which give rise to the trend and which create a different "normal" from time to time. (Schultz, 1938, p. 68)

However, fitting a trend line to time series is not a simple matter. In his study on deriving a demand curve for sugar, Schultz (1928) chose a cubic trend curve among six different functional forms on the ground that the

---

[2] Schultz preferred the method of link relatives to the method of relative changes. The method of link relatives takes the ratio of the given year's value to that of the preceding year. Thus, link relatives are always positive numbers, and this is an advantage when it is desirable to work with the logarithms. See Schultz (1928, p. 32).

highest correlation between the trend ratios was obtained when this choice was made. This correlation criterion for choosing a trend line is not obvious and was sometimes criticized.[3]

Another method of removing the time trend that gained greater popularity among empirical workers than trend ratios or link relatives was developed by Persons (1924) of the Harvard school. This method takes the residuals, instead of trend ratios, from the least squares trend regressions.[4] For the selection of a functional form of trend, Persons strongly preferred a straight line to nonlinear curves, because nonlinear trends do not have any significant economic meaning. Later researchers, like Metzler (1940), combined these two methods. They chose a functional form that gave the highest correlation between trend residuals, while not insisting on the linear trends.

Once the trend is removed from the data, the next step is to regress the demand curve. The regression methods used by Moore and Schultz were the multiple-correlation and "line of best fit" methods. Moore used the multiple-correlation method, which is referred to as "multivariate linear regression" in today's textbook terminology, in the hope of deriving a "dynamic law of demand in its complex form." Schultz, however, recognizing measurement errors prevalent in the economic data, preferred the "line of best fit" method to the least squares method. The line of best fit method will be discussed in some detail in the next section. Using their respective methods, Moore and Schultz actually did much empirical work in deriving demand curves for various agricultural products.

During the 1930s, although the idea of deriving empirical demand curves was gaining popularity among researchers, it was not without critics. In her review of Leontief's and Schultz's methods of deriving demand curves, Gilboy (1931) claimed that Schultz's method failed to specify the supply curve, and thus the price-quantity points on the scatter diagram could not be a demand curve. In addition, she charged that Schultz's empirical demand curve was not dynamic but static on the ground that a successful detrending might remove all the dynamic elements.[5]

[3] This will be discussed in detail in the section on the econometric approach to business cycles.

[4] In a sense, the Persons method and trend ratios are equivalent. In terms of logarithms, the trend ratios are exactly those residuals taken from the trend regression. Thus, the choice between these two methods can be reduced to a choice between a linear and a log-linear functional form.

[5] Moore believed that, although a demand curve derived by the method of simple correlation was static, the method of multiple correlation would provide a dynamic demand curve. Here he seemed to be confused by the assumption of *ceteris paribus*. "All other things" might include the effect of both time shifts and the prices of other goods and income. A multiple regression using the successfully

For the price theorist, it was also difficult to accept Moore and Schultz's empirical demand curves. As Stigler (1939) wrote, "Statistical demand curves are frankensteins over which he has little if any control" (p. 470). Stigler insightfully pointed out that economic theory and statistical practice in the case of demand curves are virtually independent and that this independence is attributable to the fact that theoretical studies have been both too general and too narrow. They have been too general because theoretical demand studies are general equilibrium studies in which "we sacrifice content to formal generality until we achieve the state of the perfect dilettante, and know nothing about everything" (p. 471). Moreover, they have been too narrow because they exclude variables of great importance in empirical demand analysis. In this regard, Stigler criticizes the practice of using the price index number, which is related to the problem of detrending. He claims that the practice is plausible only if all prices vary at the same rate; if not, the practice fails to capture the effect of relative price changes on the consumer's behavior caused by absolute price changes. Here he seems to recognize a deficiency of price theory, which treats money as neutral and ignores the causal link between the general price level and relative price changes. Furthermore, Stigler notes that "demand theory has been restricted to stationary conditions, and in particular anticipatings of future prices have been ruled out" (p. 473). Realizing that a wide gap exists between price theory and empirical demand analysis from the viewpoint of the theorist, Stigler concludes, "We do not know what confidence to attach to the empirical results of even a properly conducted statistical investigation" (p. 477).[6]

Some related statistical issues

A difficulty faced by econometricians in the 1920s and 1930s was that of interpreting the residuals of regressions. There were two different viewpoints on this problem, one blaming the residuals on measurement errors, the other on disturbances in variables. The former position was parallel to "that of the physical scientist who views the irregular fluctuations as being quite apart from the phenomena under observation and arising solely from

detrended data would capture the effect of other prices and income, but not the effect of time shifts. Thus, the derived demand curve cannot be dynamic. Moore's mistake seemed to be unconsciously repeated by Schultz.

[6] Stigler's view on the role of statistical research is interesting: "It must be remembered that statistical demand curves are published *because* they do not violate our theoretical preconceptions, and therefore they give a specious authenticity to these statistical products." (Stigler, 1939, p. 481). Therefore, statistical research is a servant of theory!

inaccuracies of measurement and experimental techniques" (Eisenhart, 1939, pp. 163–4). Its advocates believed that, if observations were free of measurement errors, then inferring the true relation from the observations would be nothing but a mathematical problem, which would be much easier if economic theory provided some *a priori* knowledge about the true relation.[7] Unfortunately economic data are intrinsically subject to measurement error; but there should be a way to overcome this problem. The method proposed was the least squares method, which was developed as a mean of approximate representation and thus belongs to mathematics in general, and not exclusively to statistics.[8] It was a popular method among econometricians.

The least squares method presented another difficult problem, however, in that there were two lines of best fit, one obtained by choosing x as the independent variable, the other by choosing y as the independent variable when fitting a straight line on the (x, y) scatter diagram. The problem becomes more complicated when both variables are subject to error. In this case, a trivial solution is to select the measurement-error-free variable as the independent variable and the variable subject to error as the dependent variable (Allen, 1939). When both variables are subject to measurement error, however, neither regression line by the least squares method can be the best fit, and therefore the true relationship among the variables is not deducible.

Clearly, an alternative to the least squares method had to be found. The one suggested in this context was the orthogonal regression (or line of best fit) method developed by Adcock and K. Pearson. This method "defines the line of best fit as the one for which the sum of the squares of the normal deviates of N observed points from the line becomes a minimum" (Wald, 1940, p. 284). A common objection to the orthogonal regression method was that the resultant regression line was not invariant under the scale changes of the coordinates. Furthermore, the presence of measurement errors in both variables again made it impossible to place any confidence in estimated coefficients.

---

[7] Kalman (1982) presents the "fundamental uniqueness theorem of realization theory": If the data are exact and complete, there is a unique (canonical) realization. Simply put, this theorem claims that, if the data are without noise (exact) and if they are really generated by a model (complete), then the model can be uniquely recovered from the data.

[8] The least squares method does not belong in the genuine sphere of statistics, for it does not require any assumptions about distribution of error terms. In fact, it is dealt with in numerical analysis, a field of mathematics. This method is essentially about finding an approximate representation of given observations.

Several improved methods for taking account of measurement errors were proposed. For example, Roos (1937) suggested a generalized orthogonal method that included many previous methods as special cases. The method essentially involves giving weights to the measurement errors of the variables involved and then minimizing the weighted sum of errors to get the best fit.

Schultz (1928), aware of the data deficiency of economic time series, employed both the orthogonal regression and the revised weighted sum method. The latter method also had a shortcoming in that "the fitted straight line cannot be determined without a priori assumptions (independent of the observations) regarding the weights of errors in the variables x and y" (Wald, 1940, p. 285). That is, without knowledge of the size of measurement errors a priori, there is no way of determining the true regression, and the observed values of x and y do not reveal anything about the measurement errors.

Moreover, this line of development was plagued by a more general problem: It was recognized that even a multiple regression could not include all the variables that influenced the dependent variable, and the effect of these omitted variables, as well as measurement errors, might be reflected to some degree in the regression residual. The recognition of the omission of variables was a turning point in the history of econometrics, eventually leading to the publication of Haavelmo's (1944) paper. Two distinct approaches to this problem were developed: the mechanical approach and the probability approach. The former was represented by Frisch and, to some degree, Wald, and the latter by Koopmans, Tinbergen, and Haavelmo.[9]

The advocates of the mechanical approach understand the omitted variables in the context of measurement errors. That is to say, if a multiple regression includes all the relevant variables and the involved variables are free of measurement error, one will come up with an "exact" true relation. This, however, is not always true, and thus one might end up with a spurious relationship from the multiple regression, for the errors, so far understood solely as an inaccuracy in measurement, include the effects of omitted variables, and these omitted variables somehow cause correlation between the errors. For example, consider the regression of the demand for gasoline on its price, purchasing power, road mileage, and taxes.[10] The first three would have errors that are correlated due to the omission of factors

[9] Among today's econometric schools, Hendry's seems to be close to the mechanical approach. In Hendry and Mizon (1985), error terms are interpreted according to the tradition of measurement errors.

[10] The example is drawn from Roos (1937).

affecting all three – for example, trend variables in economic time series like the population and the general price level. Because of this omission of the trend variables, the multiple regression fails to recover the true relations among the variables included.

In this context, Frisch (1934a) discussed "the fact that in statistical regression analysis there exists a great danger of obtaining nonsensical results whenever one includes in one and the same regression equation a set of variates that contains two, or more, *subsets* which are already – taken by themselves – highly intercorrelated" (p. 5). In other words, when there are some other relationships among the independent and dependent variables in a multiple regression, that is, when the true model, which involves several equations, is condensed to a single equation, there is a good chance that the coefficients of the multiple regression are spurious. This is known as a multicollinearity problem. As a method of handling the problem, Frisch proposed confluence analysis (the bunch map method), which took its cue from the fact that the less subject to error the variables in the (x, y) scatter diagram are, the closer the two possible regression lines become (one choosing x as the dependent variable and another choosing y as the dependent variable). Therefore, if an added variable helps to make these two regression lines closer, one might have confidence in the added variable and vice versa. Here it is worth noting that, although Frisch took the direction of improving the single-equation regression method, he did recognize the existence of system or multiple relations behind the multicollinearity problem.

Another approach stemming from the recognition of omitted variables was the probability approach, which is closely related to the view that accounted for errors by pointing out disturbances in variables. This approach "attributes a large portion of the apparent irregularity of their observation to a real variability which is an essential part of the phenomena studied" (Eisenhart, 1939, p. 164). It follows that, even if observations are free of measurement error, the real disturbance caused by an infinite number of individual factors is still included in the observation and the regression residual reflects the effects of this infinite number of causal factors.

At this stage, the difference in views on errors would make little difference in the practice of statistical work. Neither view was contradicted by the statistical techniques employed at that time, such as the least squares methods, the line of best fit method, or detrending. Furthermore, when the importance of omitted variables in regressions was recognized, the difference seemed to be insignificant, for the idea of a statistical test was not seriously considered among econometricians in the 1920s, and their main concern remained the measurement of theoretical relations. This became popular only after the introduction of sampling theory. For the purpose of measuring theoretical relations, either view was admissible.

One fundamental difference remained, however; the conception of a disturbance in variables was only a step away from the introduction of probability distribution into econometric analysis. It was a logical extension that, if an observation included a random element caused by an infinite number of factors, and if one saw that the cognitive limitation would keep one from recognizing all of these factors, then one might suspect that the random element followed its own laws and one would use the laws of probability to one's benefit. In the history of econometrics, the introduction of probability theory provided an alternative method of estimation – the maximum likelihood method – as well as the idea of statistical testing. Furthermore, the recognition of omitted variables led to the idea of an economic system, in particular the simultaneous-equation system, and at this juncture the maximum likelihood method seemed suitable for handling the system. A synthesis of the probabilistic and simultaneous-equation system approaches was achieved by Haavelmo (1943, 1944).

Simultaneous relationships

H. L. Moore (1914) reported a new type of demand curve for pig iron, the slope of which was positive. Instead of treating his finding as an exceptional case, he claimed that the "dogma of the uniformity of the law of demand was an idol of the static state" (p. 113) and his demand curve for pig iron was an example of dynamic demand curves. An explanation of this odd demand curve was later presented by Working (1927), who argued that what Moore found might be a law of supply rather than of demand. Working's basic idea was that a point on the price-quantity scatter diagram is the point at which supply and demand curves meet, and thus whether a fitted curve approximates a demand or a supply curve depends on the relative variability of demand and supply. Therefore, for example, if the supply curve shows a tendency to shift much farther than the demand curve, the fitted line is likely to be the demand curve. Furthermore, the price-quantity points on the scatter diagram can be said to lie on the demand curve alone (a) if supply can be disregarded as a determining factor or (b) if it is known that the demand curve has remained stable during the period under consideration and that the supply curve alone has moved (Gilboy, 1931). The first condition would hold in the case of monopolistic products, and the second condition in the case of agricultural products whose supply was subject to wide fluctuations due to the weather.

The discovery of these two conditions was the earliest form of the "identification problem," which was later systematically elaborated by Koopmans. Working's recognition of the supply and demand relations in deriving an empirical demand curve had a significant influence on empirical demand curve analysis. First, several new methods of deriving empirical demand curves taking into account the interrelations between supply and demand were suggested. Second, the identification problem was further exploited by means of mathematical techniques.

It was Leontief (1929) who developed a new method based on the idea of the interconnectedness of the supply and demand curves. Although his method did not become popular and had some statistical problems, it clearly showed the importance of a theoretical consideration of the supply and demand relation in deriving the empirical demand curve. The method was "that the demand could be fitted by minimizing the sum of square deviations in the direction parallel to the supply curve, and that the supply curve could similarly be fitted by minimizing the sum of squared deviations in a direction parallel to the demand curve" (Christ, 1967, p. 161). However, this principle allowed an infinite number of pairs of fitted equations. In order to correct for this, Leontief divided the sample into two parts and chose the unique set of equations that belonged to both periods. The demand curve obtained, however, was critically dependent on the manner of dividing the sample and the assumption that demand shifts are uncorrelated with supply shifts.[11]

It can be said that Leontief's method, although unsuccessful, represented a way of fully incorporating theoretical considerations into statistical inferences from the data. The fact that the method starts from such explicit theoretical restrictions as the constant coefficients over time, uncorrelated shifts, and the simultaneous determination of supply and demand is notable regardless of the adequacy of these theoretical restrictions, and it exemplifies the econometric methodology that approaches the economic data deductively from a definite theoretical foundation. The same spirit, Leontief's emphasis on theory in doing econometrics, characterized the Cowles Commission approach.

Another line of development that was inspired by Working's emphasis on simultaneous relationships concentrated on the identification problem. Working (1927) discussed a simple case of demand curve identification under the assumption that the supply and demand curves shifted indepen-

---

[11] In fact, Frisch (1934b) and Marschak (1934) also recognize these points. Frisch notes that effort should be concentrated on the study of the intercorrelation between shifts of demand and supply curves, indicating his research direction – confluence analysis.

dently and at random.[12] Metzler (1940), starting from Working's idea, analyzed the following four types of supply or demand shifts: (a) The curves remain fixed; (b) the curves shift in a regular manner; (c) the curves shift in a random manner; (d) the curves shift in both random and regular manners. He then classified the sixteen possible cases into three categories: indeterminate, meaningless, and identifiable. The conclusion he reached is basically the same as that of Working: "Similarly, we found that the methods yield accurate supply elasticities where supply shifts are regular while demand shifts are 'random'" (Metzler, 1940, p. 149).

Furthermore, he seemed to realize that the identification problem was quite distinct from the selection of an estimation method when he wrote that "inaccurate elasticities do not arise primarily from a failure to adopt the correct method [of estimation], but from the fact that the underlying demand and supply shifts do not correspond to those implied in the analysis" (p. 149). Thus, he emphasized the importance of knowing the data at hand for the identification problem. "In all cases it probably will be necessary to depend upon a knowledge of the industry under consideration as a test of the 'reasonableness' of the shift assumptions implied in the study" (p. 149).

Hindsight suggests that, although econometricians at that time recognized that the identification problem was quite distinct from the estimation problem, they did not link the identification problem with the model specification problem. Rather, they seemed to consider the identification problem as one that was linked to the very nature of the data at hand. Yet they did not pursue this idea.

Haavelmo's 1943 paper

A turning point in the history of econometrics occurred in 1943 when Haavelmo introduced the probability approach to econometrics. Haavelmo's

---

[12] Working (1927) also understood the nature of the conditional forecast and the reduced-form forecast. "In case of correlated shifts of the demand and supply curves, a fitted curve cannot be considered to be the demand curve for the article. It cannot be used, for example, to estimate what change in price would result from the levying of tariff upon the commodity" (p. 227). Since the fitted curve is the reduced form of supply and demand equations, it is useless for the conditional forecast of the effects of tariff levying. Correctly used, such a curve would be confined to the reduced-form forecast. "Even if the shifts of the supply and demand curves are correlated, a curve which is fitted to the points of intersection will be useful for the purposes of price forecasting, provided no new factors are introduced which did not affect the price during the period of the study" (p. 227).

scheme is composed of two main ideas: the conception of probability and the simultaneous-equation system.

Rejecting the possibility of establishing an exact relation among economic variables, Haavelmo (1943) urged the stochastical formulation of economic theories:

The necessity of introducing "error terms" in economic relations is not merely a result of statistical errors of measurement. It is as much a result of the very nature of economic behavior, its dependence upon an enormous number of factors, as compared with which we can account for, explicitly, in our theory. We need a stochastical formulation to make simplified relations elastic enough for applications. (p. 1)

In other words, the necessity of introducing error terms is a result of both measurement errors and errors in variables, but the errors in variables are probabilistic by nature; thus, certain stochastical properties can be ascribed to the error terms.

Haavelmo then emphasizes the statistical implications of the idea that a system of seemingly independent economic variables is simultaneously fulfilled by the data:

If one assumes that the economic variables considered satisfy, simultaneously, several stochastic relations, it is usually *not* a satisfactory method to try to determine each of the equations separably from the data, without regard to the restrictions which the *other* equations might impose upon the same variables. That this is so is almost self evident, for in order to prescribe a meaningful method of fitting an equation to the data, it is necessary to define the stochastical properties of *all* the variables involved. . . . Otherwise, we shall not know the meaning of the statistical results obtained. (p. 2)

For example, consider the case of estimating a demand function while ignoring the supply function. Here, the price-quantity data are the intersection points of the supply and demand curves. If one estimates the demand curve from the data without specifying the supply curve, what one is actually doing is estimating the reduced-form equation of the supply and demand, which is by no means the demand equation estimation.[13]

Frisch's view on the subject differed from Haavelmo's. As is well known, he very much opposed the probability approach. One of the main reasons for his objection to the infusion of classical sampling theory is that sampling theory is useless, even misleading, when one is dealing with the multicollinearity problem in multiple regressions (Frisch, 1934a). This is so because, even if the regression coefficients pass the test of the classical sampling error method, the resultant regression might still have the multicollinearity problem and thus represent spurious relations. That is,

[13] Working also recognized this point at a very intuitive level. See the preceding subsection.

the t-test is irrelevant in the presence of multicollinearity. However, this sort of reasoning is possible only when one assumes the multiple regression of a single equation instead of the simultaneous-equation regression. Although Frisch clearly states that the multicollinearity problem occurs theoretically (ignoring measurement errors) when a system of equations is condensed to a single equation, it is unclear why he chose not the simultaneous-equation approach but the single-equation approach (Frisch 1934a). He might have thought that a full specification of a statistically significant system of equations was virtually impossible.

Frisch's setting of the problem based on the nonprobabilistic and single-equation approach led to his development of confluence analysis and was later related to the development of the instrumental variable method.

Haavelmo, in contrast, taking the probabilistic and simultaneous-equation approach, suggested the maximum likelihood method as a substitute for the least squares method, because the latter was not suitable for introducing the concepts of probability (e.g., it did not assume any particular probability distribution of error terms) and it was also vulnerable to problems stemming from the estimation of a system.[14] That the maximum likelihood method explicitly relied on the *a priori* assumption of probability distribution implied a possible new role for econometrics; the introduction of probability permitted statistical tests of theoretical statements. Considering the desire of economists to construct empirical, refutable, and testable theories, the introduction of the probability approach was a significant event in the development of econometrics. Today, the objective of econometrics can no longer be captured by a phrase like "estimating coefficients;" one must add the phrase "testing a hypothesis."

Empirical analysis of business cycles

Decomposition of time series

A fundamental assumption of any business cycle study is that economic time series "repeat themselves through a certain historical period and under varying conditions" (Kuznets, 1928, p. 398). Without this assumption or belief, economic data would merely be records of "events that took place within specific, unrepeatable conditions of space and time" (p. 398). Every event would have to be treated as a unique incident, and a historical study of a chain of such events could at best elaborate a historical pattern of changes of events that might never again occur. This sort of study would be suitable for traditional economic history.

---

[14] This will be dealt with at length in the section on the econometric approach to business cycles.

In contrast, business cycle theorists believed that time series repeat themselves owing to the presence of unchanging laws in the economy that generate the recurrence of certain economic events in time series. In particular, the existence of cyclical fluctuations was taken as evidence of such laws. As a result, empirical business cycle analyses were, from the beginning, concerned mainly with the problem of sorting out the cycle component of time series. Once the cycle component was distinguished from the other components of the time series, the next step would be causally explaining cycles or forecasting economic conditions. But the decomposition of time series was not to be an easy task. Even though researchers largely agreed that the main components of time series were the trend, season fluctuations, and cyclical fluctuations, none of the proposed statistical decomposition methods was accepted unequivocally.

A method that was popular until it failed to forecast the Great Depression was the "Harvard barometer," constructed mainly by W. M. Persons (1924). The method consists of two parts: first, the measurement and elimination of seasonal variation and secular trend from each series under investigation and, second, the measurement of the correlation between the two series. In order to measure seasonal variations, in the case of monthly data the link relatives are calculated on a monthly basis. Then the median of the link relatives for the same month but different years are calculated. Finally, the medians are adjusted so as to make the mean of the revised relatives 100. These final figures are the adjusted monthly indices of seasonal variation. The secular trend is measured by fitting a straight line, as described in the preceding section. By the use of these measures for seasonal variation and secular trend, the original time series can be revised and, ideally, the revised time series will contain only cyclical fluctuations and irregular or unsystematic fluctuations.

It is now possible to compare the cyclical variations of two or more adjusted series. To do so: "First, compute the coefficient of correlation for the pairs of items which, according to inspection of the charts, appear to be most highly correlated; and, second, compute other coefficients for lags of both greater and less amount. When some pairing gives a higher coefficient than adjacent pairings, the degree of lag for maximum correlation is indicated" (Persons, 1924, pp. 161–2).[15] The lags between various possible

---

[15] Persons, however, warns against an abuse of the coefficient of correlation method. He argues that the standard errors of coefficients of correlation do not have the usual meaning implied by the classical theory of probability, because, first, "any past period that we select for study is . . . a special period with characteristics distinguishing it from the other periods, and so cannot be considered a 'random' selection; second, the individual items of the series are not chosen independently, but they constitute a *group* of successive items with a

pairs of time series are then used as a basis for forecasting the economic condition.[16]

However, an important objection raised by Roos (1934) to the idea of decomposing time series could not be ignored:

In examining time series, it is of paramount importance to take all major factors into account. . . . If all important factors are taken into account, the influence of the many neglected but minor factors (all economic quantities are related) should give a net constant effect ("systemetic error", in the theory of the adjustment of observations). If the analysis is complete, there will be only random residuals left. The use of a trend in correlation analysis is therefore a confession of ignorance of fundamental factors involved. (p. 250)

Although Roos's criticism is directed at the practice of detrending, it also implies that the empirical business cycle studies represented by Persons's approach generally fail to provide, or ignore, causal explanations of business cycle phenomena. They are "the result of discussing [important] factors without identifying them" (Roos, 1934, p. 4). The argument that empirical economic analyses remained at a level of naive empiricism was tantamount to the view that business cycle theory had no role in the empirical analyses of cycles. Roos interpreted the trend as "the influence of the many neglected but minor factors." In Moore and Schultz's view, it reflected dynamic elements that shift a static curve. Some economists thought that the trend was a part of long waves, like a Kondratief cycle (see Kuznets, 1928). In any case, these different interpretations of the notion of trend at least revealed the lack of a received causal explanation.

Furthermore, the belief that the statistical decomposition of time series was a meaningless problem was evidence of a deep and wide gulf between theory and empirical studies on business cycles. Haberler (1963), for instance, pointed out such a gap from the viewpoint of a theorist:

The question is . . . : How to separate the effects of the causes responsible for the cycle from the effects of the causes responsible for the trend. The further assumption is made that two sets of effects are additive. This assumption is surely unwarranted. . . . As a consequence, if we could make the experiment of abstracting from the actual system which is subject to the joint operation of both sets of causes, first those that make for cycles, and second those that make for trend, the

characteristic conformation" (Persons, 1924, pp. 162–3). For these reasons, he seems to rely in practice more on graphical comparison of the cycle charts than on the coefficient of correlation method. In fact, Persons's view had been taken throughout the 1920s and 1930s as an authoritative ground for rejecting the introduction of probability theory into analyses of time series.

[16] This method is very similar to the idea behind the "reference cycles" postulated by the National Bureau of Economic Research. One procedure common to both is the search for empirical regularities of *leads and lags* relationships among different time series.

sum of the two effects would not be equal to, but would probably greatly exceed the total observed change. (p. 458n)

Haberler's intuition was that there might be an important causal relation between trend and cycle and thus these two sets could not be additive. In any event, it was obvious that the statistical decomposition of time series suffered from a lack of theoretical justification. In addition, the statistical techniques employed were unsatisfactory for attacking the decomposition problem. The latter were exemplified by the spectral analysis of time series. It was well known that Fourier's theorem provides a transformation of time series to frequency, and the inference in the frequency domain makes it possible to decompose the time series according to their length of cycle. Although spectral analysis (or, as it is often called, "harmonic analysis") is theoretically perfect – a fact that attracted many economists' attention[17] – deficiencies of economic data, such as small sample size and the lack of an appropriate estimation method in the frequency domain, prevented it from being introduced on a wide scale into econometrics.

Propagation mechanism and external shocks

Along with Persons's method of decomposing time series without the help of economic theory, there was an approach in the 1920s and 1930s that involved generating cyclical movements in the form of mathematical functions. This field was called "quantitative business cycle theory" by Tinbergen and "macrodynamics" by Frisch. The aim of quantitative business cycle theory is to formulate a system of economic relations that generates the cyclical movements of the variables involved. That is to say, this class of cycle theory might be looked upon as an attempt to find a system of equations whose solutions reveal cycle-like movements. The solutions are in the form of differential and difference equations. This way of looking at cyclical fluctuations of time series is essentially borrowed from classical physics, which is concerned mainly with deriving differential equations that approximate the orbit of a planet.

There are two main ways of formulating a system, both of which were first articulated in the 1930s (see Haavelmo, 1940). One is to consider the system of relations as exact equations without error terms. The resulting solution is an error-free difference and/or differential equation whose time expansion is wavelike. In the context of business cycle theory, this way of formulating a system is in line with endogenous cycle theory: Cyclical fluctuations are due mainly to the inherent characteristics of the economic

---

[17] For example, Friedman spent two years on spectral analysis, but failed to gain any advantage from it. See R. D. Friedman (1976).

system, and exogenous shocks to the system have little effect on cyclical movements. Examples are Kalecki (1935) and Hicks's (1950) floor and ceiling model.

Kalecki (1935), whose work was originally published in Polish in 1933, used the production lag and the accumulation of capital to generate a periodic movement. In addition to the fact that Kalecki's system does not introduce shocks as a cause of cycles, it has two remarkable features. First, it is based on the notion of capital goods production. Second, a very small number of variables is sufficient to generate cyclical movement. Although general business cycle theory emphasizes the importance of monetary variables, prices do not appear in Kalecki's system. Nonetheless, the system is capable of producing business cycles. This achievement is remarkable considering the complexity and diversity of cycle theories available at that time. Here one can detect an implicit belief among quantitive cycle theorists that, even though the reality seems complicated, its underlying system might be quite simple, like physical laws.

Another way of formulating a system of economic relations is to make a distinction between the economic mechanism and the external shocks operating on that mechanism. The idea that cycles can be obtained by successively summing and successively differencing a pure random process was first presented clearly by Slutsky in 1927.[18] This idea was innovative because it opened the possibility of perceiving cycle phenomena as a result of continuous random shocks. In the extreme, it followed from this possibility that the cyclical fluctuations in time series could be a statistical artifact obtained by an arbitrary and economically meaningless process of summations and differencings.[19] It was at this juncture that Frisch set up a conceptual framework in which cycles were generated but the process of summation and differencing acquired definite economic meaning. He put the problem in this way:

The most important feature of the free oscillations is that the length of the cycles and the tendency toward dampening are determined by the intrinsic structure of the swinging system, while the intensity (the amplitude) of the fluctuations is determined primarily by the exterior impulse. An important consequence of this is that a more or less regular fluctuation may be produced by a cause which operates irregularly. . . . This fact has frequently been overlooked in economic cycle analysis. (Frisch, 1933, p. 155)

---

[18] An English version of Slutsky's paper of 1927 was published in *Econometrica* in 1937. See Slutsky (1937).

[19] In fact, Sargent (1979) argues that Kuznets's twenty-year-cycle is clearly a statistical artifact. He shows that Kuznets's long waves "are something induced in the data by the transformation applied and not really a characteristic of the

If cyclical phenomena are understood from this point of view, one has to distinguish the propagation mechanism from the impulse. "The propagation problem is the problem of explaining by the structural properties of the swinging system what the character of the swing would be in case the system was started in some initial situation" (Frisch, 1933, p. 155)

The propagation mechanism in the absence of external shocks would be damping oscillations, which eventually die away. External shocks, however, drive the system to cyclical fluctuations. Therefore, it is "possible to explain observed cyclical movements by the combination of a structure which is noncyclic, but which contains inertial forces, and outside influences of random events" (Haavelmo, 1940, p. 321). The main objectives of the cycle analysis in this connection would be the theoretical underpinning of the propagation mechanism, or structure, and the statistical determination of its parameters.

Frisch's framework, which distinguishes the propagation mechanism from the impulse, became a cornerstone in the development of empirical business cycle analysis. The wide acceptance of this framework among empirical cycle researchers is partially responsible for the shift of research interest from the conventional analysis of the visual shape of cycles, such as their amplitude, periodicity, and turning point, to the statistical determination of the hidden parameters of the propagation mechanism. Although one should admit the influence of the historical fact that cycles became mild after the Second World War, it is quite possible that the Frisch approach to cyclical phenomena made conventional cycle analysis less interesting, because cyclical fluctuations that are described by observed amplitudes and periodicity can be directly derived, at least theoretically, if the hidden but true parameters of the propagation mechanism are statistically uncovered. As Koopmans (1949) explains it:

In models employing a system of linear difference equations, it was found that the period and degree of damping of the cycle movement . . . are determined by the numerical values of the parameters (coefficients and lags) of the structural equations, whereas the amplitude and phase of the cycle movement . . . at any given time are determined by initial conditions and by subsequent external influences, systematic or random. (p. 65)

Today's economists, such as Sargent, echo Koopmans's conclusion.[20]

economic system" (p. 251). Thus, of importance is the theoretical meaning of the data transformation method or of the process of summation and differencing.

[20] Frisch's framework, however, has not been free of criticism. Blatt (1978, 1980) argues that the Frischian approach cannot properly describe and explain the stylized, though not well established, fact of cycles – the asymmetry of the cycle. For recent discussions of the asymmetry of the cycle, see Neftci (1984), DeLong and Summers (1984), and Blanchard and Watson (1984).

Acknowledging the importance of Frisch's framework, Sargent (1979) argues:

If the initial conditions of low-order deterministic linear difference equations are subjected to repeated random shocks of a certain kind, there emerges the possibility of recurring, somewhat irregular cycles of the kind seemingly infesting economic data. This is an important idea that is really the foundation of macroeconometric models, an idea that was introduced into economics by Slutsky (1937) and Frisch (1933). (p. 219)

Econometric approach to business cycles

Background of the Cowles Commission method

Although the simultaneous relationship of demand and supply was recognized by Working as early as 1927, its equivalent in business cycle analysis, the concept of building an economic structure, was not employed in empirical business cycle studies until the late 1930s. Tinbergen (1939) made the first attempt to use the conception of structure in empirical business cycle studies.[21] He specified the structure with many individual equations, each of which represents an indispensable economic relation. At least one of these equations must be dynamic in the sense that it includes lags. Moreover, the structure should be a "complete system"; that is, the number of equations included should equal the number of endogenous variables. The coefficients of the system are derived by estimating individual equations separately using a detrending process and the least squares method. Once numerical values for coefficients are derived, the complete system is solved to get the final-form equations.[22]

The coefficients and the final-form equations of the complete system, then, are used in policy analysis and testing of economic theory. Measures of policy can be grouped as "(a) changes in the coefficients or lags, or both, i.e., changes in the economic structure of society - e.g., price-stabilizing measures, (b) shocks - e.g., the Veterans' bonus payment in the United States in 1936, (c) changes in the average level of some variable - e.g., minimum wage legislation" (Tinbergen, 1939, vol. 2, p. 166). One can analyze the effect of business cycle policy by looking at the final form. If a policy reduces the degree of

---

[21] Note that Tinbergen's conception of structure corresponds exactly to Frisch's propagation mechanism, discussed in the preceding section.

[22] The final form of the complete system is an equation relating the endogenous variable to its own lagged endogenous variables and exogenous variables, whereas the reduced-form equation relates the endogenous variable to its own *and* other lagged endogenous variables in the system and exogenous variables. Thus, the final-form equation is formally nothing but an ordinary linear stochastic difference equation.

damping and the amplitude of the final form, that policy is acceptable, and vice versa. For testing of theories, the multiple-correlation method tells econometricians which set of variables has the greatest explanatory power. Each set of explanatory variables can be deduced from a different theory. Hence, the selection of variables directly implies a selection among competing theories.[23]

Tinbergen's work might be considered a rather bold attempt to explore policy analysis and testing by means of econometrics. In many respects, however, his work can also be interpreted as an attempt to set the problems to be solved by later researchers, giving them a direction to follow. For example, his discomfort with the autonomy of the complete system is still an unresolved problem for today's economists. Tinbergen pointed out the possibility that a change in consumption, technical progress, or policy would change the coefficients of the other equations in the system. "Hence it is not sure beforehand that a change in one coefficient will leave all other coefficients as they are: some coefficients may be linked to one another by relations into which we did not inquire" (Tinbergen, 1939, vol. 2, p. 167). The problem of achieving the autonomy of the system has been one of the most critical in the development of econometrics. Such controversies as the reduced-form estimation versus the structural-equation estimation, the Lucas critique of the structural-equation method, and Sims's counterattack on the rational expectations school all more or less revolve around the issue of the autonomy of the system. Furthermore, Tinbergen's incomplete and sometimes incorrect methods were placed on econometricians' agenda of problems to be solved. The use of lags without firm theoretical foundations, the naive system of equations called the "arrow" model, which does not adopt the idea of the simultaneous determination of economic relations, and a lack of clarification in policy analysis were all difficulties that had to be resolved by later economists.[24] Eventually, many of these

---

[23] This type of testing is, of course, naive in many respects. First, it assumes a straightforward deducibility of the econometric model from descriptive economic theory. As is known, the validity of such an assumption is hardly guaranteed on any ground, and there always exist such dangers as the Bayesian bias and specification errors. Furthermore, even if such a deducibility is assumed to be possible, testing based on the comparison of explanatory powers is not robust with respect to sample size and sample selection procedure. Tinbergen's type of testing is not based on the concept of probability and, thus, cannot be said to be stochastic. Rather his testing procedure is much similar to today's "stepwise" estimation.

[24] Interestingly, Haavelmo pointed out several deficiencies in Tinbergen's work. Although Haavelmo was a strong supporter of Tinbergen's approach, he did show, for example, that the conventional t-test is not sufficient to decide whether the rate of interest plays only a minor role, if the model has a severe

problems were solved or considered to have been solved by the Cowles Commission. Between Tinbergen (1939) and the Cowles Commission, however, lay the work of Mann and Wald (1943) and Haavelmo (1944).

Mann and Wald (1943) dealt with the theoretical problems of econometrics that would occur in estimating structural equations by the maximum likelihood method. They showed that, even if observations are not independent, the estimates of the coefficients of linear stochastic difference-equation systems[25] are consistent and their asymptotic distributions are normal.[26] They also clarified the cases in which the ordinary least squares (OLS) estimator gives asymptotically unbiased estimates, thus providing substantial justification for the use of OLS when the disturbance term is serially independent. Furthermore, by distinguishing the problem of coefficient estimation from that of prediction, they clearly delineated the cases in which estimating the coefficients of the system is impossible, although prediction is still possible by use of the reduced form. This, as they proved, calls for the introduction of additional *a priori* information. In other words, Mann and Wald demonstrated the statistical necessity of theoretical restrictions in the estimation of the coefficients of the simultaneous-equation system, which was later called the "identification problem" and formally solved by Koopmans.

Haavelmo's work (1944) was another milestone that forged a new direction for econometrics. According to Haavelmo, econometrics aimed at the conjunction of economic theory and actual measurements. But a bridge

multicollinearity problem (Haavelmo, 1941). Haavelmo (1943) could also be interpreted as indirectly criticizing Tinbergen's use of the least squares method for the estimation of structural equations. It seems that Haavelmo's 1944 paper is a manifesto that declares the direction of econometrics, providing statistical foundations and tools for accomplishing Tinbergen's agenda of policy analysis and testing of theory.

[25] Mann and Wald's linear stochastic difference-equation system is identical with the complete dynamic simultaneous-equation system of Geweke (1978). Geweke showed that a complete static simultaneous-equation model is a special case of the complete dynamic simultaneous-equation system; i.e., lagged endogenous variables are not permitted in the former case. If the system determines the endogenous variables without any restrictions on the coefficients, the system is said to be complete. Thus, the reduced form of the complete dynamic simultaneous-equation model would correspond to the usual vector autoregression (VAR) system. The point here is that the most generalized case of the conventional simultaneous-equation model is Mann and Wald's linear stochastic difference system.

[26] It is worth noting that Mann and Wald (1943) proved for the first time the asymptotic normality of the OLS estimator, and their procedure of proof (pp. 185–90) is still standard today.

between them was never completely built. This was so because theory was not constructed in such a way that the very probabilistic nature of economic relations could be introduced and because the statistical tools used were not founded on statistical theory. Thus, what was needed included, first, a probabilistic formulation of economic theory whereby theories would be built as statistical hypotheses and, second, an explicit introduction of probability into econometric research.

Haavelmo (1944), in an argument very similar to that of Popperian falsificationism,[27] asserts that theory can be refuted by a confrontation with facts:

The model . . . becomes *an a priori hypothesis* about real phenomena, stating that every system of values that we might observe of the "true" variable will be one that belongs to the set of value-systems that is admissible within the model. The idea behind this is . . . that Nature has a way of selecting joint value-systems of the "true" variables such that these systems are as if the selection has been made by the rule defining our theoretical model. . . . It is then natural to adopt the convention that a theory is called true or false according as the hypotheses implied are true or false, when tested against the data chosen as the "true" variables. (p. 9)

This belief, that any explanation is tentative, reappears in the discussion of the autonomy of economic structure. Although Haavelmo believes that there are laws of nature, he also contends that the structure accepted by economists is essentially tentative and therefore not perfectly autonomous with respect to structural changes.[28] Thus, the problem of autonomy should be understood as one of achieving a *greater* degree of autonomy for the

[27] It is not at all clear whether he was actually familiar with Popper's writings or the literature of logical positivism in the 1930s, but his arguments are remarkably similar to those of Popper. For instance, he states that "our guard against futile speculation is the requirement that the result of our theoretical considerations are, ultimately, to be compared with some real phenomena" (Haavelmo, 1944, p. 1), which is the empiricist proposition common to both the logical positivist and Popper. However, the chosen explanation or theory is not a necessary truth. "But whatever be the 'explanations' we prefer, it is not to be forgotten that they are all our own artificial inventions in a search for an understanding of real life; they are not hidden truths to be 'discovered'" (ibid., p. 3). Or: "But will the model [which is acceptable on the basis of a certain number of observations] hold also for future observations? We cannot give any a priori reason for such a supposition. We can only say that, according to a vast record of actual experiences, it seems to have been fruitful to believe in the possibility of such empirical inductions" (ibid., p. 10). Thus, a theory or a hypothesis cannot be confirmed by facts, and the accepted one is only tentatively accepted – the chief tenet of Popperian falsificationism.

[28] Haavelmo's belief in the existence of fundamental laws of nature corresponds to Hendry's (1980) hypothesis of the DGP (data generating process).

system. For this reason, the system of simultaneous equations is definitely preferred to a single equation, since the former achieves a greater degree of autonomy by allowing less confluent relations:

Any relation that is derived by combining two or more relations within a system, we call a *confluent relation*. Such a confluent relation has, of course, usually a lower degree of autonomy (and never a higher one) than each of the relations from which it is derived, and all the more so the greater the number of different relations upon which it depends. . . . [But] how can we actually distinguish between the "original" system and a derived system of original confluence relations? (Haavelmo, 1944, p. 29)

His answer to this question is in agreement with that of Tinbergen: "The construction of systems of autonomous relations is . . . a matter of intuition and factual knowledge; it is an art" (Haavelmo, 1944, p. 29).[29]

Haavelmo then suggests that the maximum likelihood estimation method is legitimate for estimating the system of equations, for, unlike the least squares method, it explicitly assumes a particular distribution of error terms. He also suggests that the Neyman-Pearson theory of test is appropriate in this connection.

Haavelmo's scheme clearly proved the necessity of introducing the probabilistic approach into econometrics and became an essentially standard approach in econometrics, which was further encouraged and developed by the Cowles Commission.

Econometric approach to business cycles

One of the major achievements of the Cowles Commission was the conceptual clarification of the diverse theoretical studies on econometrics.[30] The members of the commission, represented and led by Koopmans, pursued the implications of the studies of Frisch, Tinbergen, Haavelmo, and others. The position they adopted was called the "econometric approach to business cycles." By accepting classical sampling theory, following Haavelmo's scheme, it was possible to introduce statistical method and theory into econometrics. And by following Frisch and Slutsky's theory of random summation, it was possible to adopt a view of cycles that differed from that of conventional descriptive cycle theories and, accordingly, a different research direction. Furthermore, Tinbergen's strong policy orientation was taken to be an objective of econometrics.

[29] Haavelmo's emphasis on the relative nature of autonomy is worth noting here. If this nature were fully appreciated, the question to pursue would naturally be "autonomous with respect to what?" and the uncharacteristic expansion of the model size in the 1950s and 1960s, which was regarded as a way of arriving at the autonomous system, might not be so popular.

[30] For the early history of the Cowles Commission, consult Christ (1952).

Other theoretical achievements of the Cowles Commission were the derivation of workable statistical inference procedures, such as the maximum likelihood estimator and the limited information maximum likelihood (LIML) estimator,[31] and the theoretical study of the properties of those procedures, such as the asymptotic properties of estimators, and comparisons among various kinds of estimators.

In retrospect, the Cowles Commission's econometric approach to business cycles can be seen as a cornerstone in the shaping of today's macroeconometrics, in the sense that it not only triggered the redirection of cycle theories, but stressed, at least formally, the need for testing economic theory.

According to Koopmans, conventional business cycle studies were concerned exclusively with the superficial characteristics of cyclical fluctuations: The majority of empirical studies concentrated on measuring such characteristics of cyclical fluctuations as periodicity and turning point. However, Koopmans (1949b) argues that it "does not become altogether clear why the cyclical forms of movement should receive such exclusive attention" (pp.164–5). Instead he claims that research should be directed toward finding the underlying economic behavior of individual agents that generates empirical regularities like cyclical fluctuations. That is to say, the attention should be shifted to "the behavior of groups of economic agents (consumers, workers, entrepreneurs, dealers, etc.) whose modes of action and response, in the social organization and technological environment of the society studied, are the ultimate determinants of the levels of economic variables as well as their fluctuations" (Koopmans, 1949b, p. 164). To achieve this end, the use of theories that are based largely on introspection and provide knowledge of the motives and actions of economic agents is indispensable. Such theories suggest the system of structural equations, which is composed of

(a) principles of economic behavior derived from general observation – partly introspective, partly through interview or experience – of the motives of economic decision, (b) knowledge of legal and institutional rules restricting individual behavior (tax schedules, price control, reserve requirements, etc.) (c) technological knowledge, and (d) carefully constructed definitions of variables. (Koopmans, 1949b, p. 125)

The economic variables whose movements we observe are said to be determined simultaneously by structural (behavioral) equations. If the measurement of structural equations is possible, observed regularities like

---

[31] See Anderson and Rubin (1949). In a sense, it can be said that Anderson and Rubin's limited information maximum likelihood (LIML) estimator was already anticipated in Koopmans's discussion of the identification problem, since the LIML method is possible only when the system is identifiable.

cyclical fluctuations can be directly explained, in the same way that Newton's law of gravitation explains Kepler's empirical regularities of planetary motion.[32] However, the realization that the measurement of structural equations would constitute a rather fundamental explanation of cyclical fluctuations suggests a path of development for cycle theories that differ from conventional cycle theories.

First, the major concern of empirical business cycle study has shifted from the measurement of the cyclical characteristics of time series to the measurement of coefficients and time lags of structural equations. That is, the new econometric approach, whereby the coefficients of structural equations are estimated from the time series data, pays less attention to cyclical characteristics such as amplitudes, phases, and turning points.

Second, unlike many interwar cycle theories, which largely attempted to present a picture of self-generating cyclical movement (i.e., the endogenous explanation of business cycles), the econometric approach offers another possible explanation: When the propagation mechanism is shocked by continuous exogenous influences, the outcome is cyclical fluctuation of time series. This implies that it is not necessary for cycle theories to explain the turning points endogenously, and in the extreme it is even possible to interpret the cyclical phenomena as a statistical artifact without content. (See Koopmans, 1941, 1949b). Although such an interpretation was not explicitly stated by any proponents of the econometric approach, one suspects that it was implicit in their thinking when they enthusiastically accepted Keynesian macroeconomics, which is by no means concerned with cyclical phenomena themselves.[33] In any event, the new direction of aggregate economics was toward a clarification of the propagation mechanism or, in the Cowles Commission's language, the structure.[34] Conse-

---

[32] The system of behavioral equations is, of course, dynamic in the sense that it contains lagged endogenous variables. Without such lags, the system cannot generate cycles.

[33] Here, as is usually granted, Keynesian economics is to be distinguished from the economics of Keynes. An emphasis on uncertainty in the *General Theory* might be interpreted as, or at least extendable to, a cycle theory, whereas its vulgarized version, American Keynesian macroeconomics, was concerned exclusively with the short-run movement of the aggregated economy, thus leaving no room for cycle theory. See Leijonhufvud (1968).

[34] In this regard, members of the Cowles Commission in its early period, especially Koopmans and Marschak, seemed to prefer as a theoretical model for the structural equations the Walrasian system, which is based on the economic decisions of an individual agent. For instance, Koopmans (1947) had Walrasian theory in mind when he defended the Cowles Commission's approach to business cycles. However, it seems that this tendency was not maintained among

quently, the interwar cycle theories became less popular in the discussion of aggregate economics, leading to a full development of Keynesian macroeconomics.

Third, efforts to build and estimate the coefficients of the simultaneous-equation system naturally led to more concrete and precise policy discussion. Given the coefficients of the stable structural equations, it was possible to predict the most probable outcome of a policy change. Through a comparison of the outcomes, the effectiveness of different policies could be evaluated. The strong inclination of economists to tackle policy problems was reinforced by this econometric approach, and in fact the belief in "fine tuning" in the 1960s was clearly related to it.

A major difficulty, however, was the stability of the structure being estimated. As Haavelmo clearly recognized, it is impossible in principle to construct a true structure that is stable over time, but for the purpose of policy evaluation, it is not impossible to build a stable structure with respect to policy changes. Koopmans seems to have used the stable structure in this limited sense (see Koopmans and Barsch, 1959). During the Cowles Commission period, however, the stability of structure, together with the multiple-hypothesis test, remained the most serious problem in the commission's program. Unfortunately, this issue did not receive any serious attention until the New Classical economics attacked Keynesian economics on the basis of the "stability of the structure" problem.

Identification problem

During the Cowles Commission era, econometrics was established as a new branch of economics. It was the Cowles Commission that defined the territory of econometrics and its relation to economic theory and elaborated the structural estimation method. Econometrics, in particular structural estimation, was believed to be a useful tool for formulating policy recommendations:

The economist can do this [estimating the results of changes that he has never observed] if his past observations suffice to estimate the relevant structural constants prevailing before the change. Having estimated the past structure the economist can estimate the effect of varying it. He can thus help to choose those variations of structure that would produce – the most desirable results. That is, he can advise on policies [of a government or firm]. (Marschak, 1950, p. 2)

The Cowles Commission's emphasis on policy as an objective of economic research perhaps goes back to Tinbergen and Frisch, who had directly

the commission members for long, and they later became inclined toward Keynesian economics. In effect, all of Klein's major empirical works employed the Keynesian system. See Klein (1950) and Klein and Goldberger (1955).

influenced the commission's direction of research, and this policy orientation was sometimes called "social engineering."[35]

Therefore, the discovery or determination of a stable economic structure is of utmost importance for the purpose of policy analysis. However, a stable structure can be determined either on the basis of economic theory or on the basis of theory combined with empirical observations. If one admits the limitation of *a priori* theory, as did the Cowles Commission and other econometricians, the latter is a natural direction to pursue. But what about statistical inference without the help of theory? "Such purely empirical relationships when discernible are likely to be due to the presence and persistence of the underlying structural relationships, and (if so) could be deduced from a knowledge of the latter" (Koopmans, 1949a, p. 126). Furthermore, it would be basically impossible to induce a structural relationship from empirical observations without additional information. Thus, the problems are "the limits to which statistical inference, from the data to the structural equation, . . . is subjected, and the manner in which these limits depend on the support received from economic theory" (Koopmans, 1949a, p. 126). This is the identification problem, which was repeatedly discussed by Frisch and Haavelmo. The identification problem, in other terms, is deciding whether it is possible to determine the structural relationship from observations and given additional information.

Suppose that a structure is described by a complete set of equations with *a priori* restrictions that are directly derived by theory.[36] Then two structures S and S^1 are "observationally equivalent," "if the two conditional distributions of endogenous variables generated by S and S^1 are identical for all possible values of exogenous variables" (Koopmans, 1949a, p. 126). And a structure S is "identifiable" if there is no other equivalent structure S^1.

In mathematical terms, in the case of linear models, the identification problem is formally equivalent to the solvability of a linear simultaneous-equation system. Hence, a necessary condition for the identification of a structural-equation system is that "the number of variables excluded from that equation (more generally: the number of linear restrictions on the

[35] The commission's view, especially that of Marschak and Koopmans, that policy making is similar to controlling a mechanical system, resembles Tinbergen's and Keynes's view on policy. See Marschak (1947). Both views were essentially interventionistic, although their roots differed. One of the reasons for the ready acceptance of Keynesianism by both the Cowles Commission and Tinbergen might be this similarity in their view on policy making. This partially explains why the Cowles Commission accepted the Keynesian system even though its key members, like Marschak and Koopmans, preferred the Walrasian theory.
[36] By a "complete set of equations," it is meant that there are as many equations as endogenous variables.

parameter of that equation) be at least equal to the number (G) of structural equations less one" (the order condition). A necessary and sufficient condition is such that "we can form at least one nonvanishing determinant of order $G-1$ out of those coefficients . . . with which the variables excluded from the structural equation appear in the $G-1$ other structural equations" (the rank condition; Koopmans, 1949a, p. 135). This rank condition is equivalent to saying that a structural equation is identifiable if it is impossible to produce the same equation by a linear combination of all equations, that is, if that equation is linearly independent.[37]

It might be said that the identification problem is a bridge linking theory and statistical inference. An ideal state is one in which theory provides a valid and identifiable structure, thereby guaranteeing statistical inference from the data to the structural equations. But normally this is not the case. Most economic theory cannot be sufficiently reduced to provide universally valid structural equations. At most, it is reducible to a class that allows several different specifications of structural equations. Therefore, an important question concerns the extent to which the specifications of the structure are subject to statistical testing and the extent to which the choice is to be taken as a matter of theory.[38] Koopmans (1949a) admits that "we do not yet have a satisfactory statistical theory of choice among several alternative hypotheses" (p. 141) and points out the need for further fundamental research on principles of statistical inference – for example,

---

[37] It was Haavelmo (1944) who discussed the identification problem in a more general functional form than the linear case. Accordingly, he approached the problem by investigating the local linear independence around a particular parameter point of the structural system. It follows that the identification problem occurs only after the parameters of the system are estimated. So he classified this problem under the heading "estimation." However, if the system is restricted to be linear, the linear independence of the system does not have to be local, and thus one can separate the identification problem from the estimation problem. Thus, Koopmans interprets this problem as a logical problem that precedes estimation. See Koopmans, Rubin, and Leipnik (1950).

[38] Somewhat differently, Friedman noted the limitation of the identification problem in the following way. According to the Cowles Commission, the choice of structure assumes two substeps: the selection of a class of admissible hypotheses from all possible hypotheses (the choice of a model) and the selection of one hypothesis from this class (the choice of a structure). The identification problem is strictly applicable to the latter substep, but it has nothing to do with the choice of model, which has to be left to some arbitrary principles, such as Occam's razor. Thus, there is a danger that the introduction of the concept of identification disguises the fundamental difficulty of recovering true relations from the data at hand. See Friedman (1953, esp. pp. 12–13) and Koopmans (1949a, p. 127).

the multiple-hypothesis test and the prevention of strong and subjective confidence in untested specifications (i.e., a Bayesian approach). Recognizing the limitations of statistical theory in the choice of specifications, Koopmans emphasizes the importance of *a priori* knowledge. Being skeptical about the exogeneity test, he notes "that the evidence on which the choice of exogenous variables rests must be sought primarily in qualitative knowledge about the place of the variables in question in the causal hierarchy, with slight chances of corroboration from statistical tests utilizing time series" (Koopmans, 1952, p. 205).

Klein's empirical work

Although the Cowles Commission during the 1940s had actively exploited the structural-equation method, its efforts were concentrated mainly on statistical theory and techniques. The results of empirical studies utilizing the structural-equation method did not parallel the theoretical achievement. Koopmans and members of the commission were not confident of the success of empirical studies because of the unsatisfactory state of both economic theory and econometrics.[39]

Klein, however, was an exception. Unlike the other members of the commission, his interest lay exclusively in the building of large-scale econometric models, and his work had been continuously subject to dispute, owing to the plain fact that his large-scale econometric models were substantial applications of the Cowles Commission's econometric approach.

In 1950, Klein developed three large-scale econometric models, the first two in his successive modelings of the U.S. economy. A larger model, called the Klein Model III, includes fifteen equations, three of which are definitional identities (Klein, 1950). Thus, there are fifteen endogenous variables, and fourteen variables are assumed to be exogenous, four of which are policy variables. Among twelve stochastic equations, four are related to the market for goods and services, another four concern the housing market, three describe the money market, and the remaining one defines the labor market. In particular, the model includes three adjustment equations, which are a function of lagged dependent variables. This model was established by the LIML method using the annual data for 1921–41.

---

[39] Explaining why the econometric approach was inconclusive in many empirical studies, Koopmans (1949b) points out four difficulties of testing the specifications of the model: (a) the lack of a multiple-hypothesis test, (b) the problem of *a priori* confidence in untested specifications, (c) the specification search based on the data given, and (d) the lack of testing of the degree of aggregation. In addition to the unsatisfactory state of econometrics, Koopmans (1949a) emphasizes the need to elaborate and consolidate economic theory.

Another model, the Klein–Goldberger (1955) model, has fifteen stochastic equations and five identities. It contains thirty-four variables, twenty of which are endogenous and fourteen of which are exogenous. The model seems to reflect its Keynesian origin by emphasizing the consumer demand aspect. The data are twenty annual observations from the periods 1929–41 and 1946–52. The method of estimation was also the LIML method.

When these models were tested, the results were not encouraging. Christ (1951) performed one test of the Klein Model III, modifying it to include the data for 1946 and 1947. He compared the forecasting performance of that model for 1948 with the performance of two naive models suggested by Friedman. The first naive model forecasts each endogenous variable for a given year by the value in the preceding year, implying no changes. The second assumes that the rate of increase to be forecast is the same as the rate one year earlier, thus implying a constant change. Christ found that the naive model forecasts were closer to the observed values in the majority of thirteen cases than were those of the Klein Model III. Christ (1956) tested the Klein-Goldberger model in a similar manner. The performance of the structural equation was superior, yet its success was not decisive compared with the naive models.

These results constituted a serious attack on the econometric approach, because Friedman's naive models are no more than guesswork that requires little time or effort.[40]

However, the tests revealed a crucial fact. That is, the structural model, which does no better than naive models in forecasting continuing growth, tends to do better in forecasting a downturn of the time series.[41] This is

---

[40] Friedman (1951), however, pretends to offer some theoretical interpretations of his naive models. According to him, the first model embodies the theory that there are no essential forces responsible for economic change, and the second embodies a theory of pure secular change that denies cyclical changes. In spite of Friedman's explanations, it seems that his models are "naive" enough to ridicule his opponents, reminding us of Columbus's egg. In addition, Friedman had already articulated the idea of testing models by comparing their forecasting ability (Friedman, 1939). In the earlier article, he compared Tinbergen's forecasts with the actual values and found the forecasts to be poor. This emphasis on predictions seemed to have developed into his instrumentalist methodology. See Friedman (1953).

[41] In contrast, it is also well known that the forecasting of the VAR model, by and large, is better than that of large-scale simultaneous-equation models, but the VAR system usually fails to forecast the turning points of business cycles. Here, one might notice intuitively the similarity between the Friedman model and the VAR system.

encouraging and justifies the effort invested in the development of the econometric approach.

Adelman and Adelman (1959) provided further encouragement under these unfavorable circumstances. They compared the long-term behavior of the Klein-Goldberger model with actual trends and cycles in the U.S. economy. Without random shocks, a linearized version of the model exhibited simple linear growth over the long run. With the addition of random shocks, however, the simulated time series exhibited cycles that were similar in length, amplitude, and timing to those historically observed. The simulated cycles also conformed well to the criteria set by the National Bureau of Economic Research, such as leads-and-lags relationships among different economic time series. Such results were also consistent with the view that cycles represent responses of the economy to exogenous random shocks, that is, the Frischian scheme of the propagation mechanism and external shocks.

In conclusion, it might be said that this testing of Klein's aggregate model reflected the validity of the propagation mechanism-shock scheme, as well as the unsatisfactory state of econometric techniques. Yet the results were encouraging enough for Koopmans (1957) to say that "it is therefore important that structural estimation and prediction and the testing of its results be continued and extended" (p. 205).

Criticisms of the econometric approach

The NBER versus the Cowles Commission

Along with the Cowles Commission, the National Bureau of Economic Research (NBER) was a leading research institution in the 1940s. Especially in the field of business cycle research, these two institutions represented different methodologies. The methodology of the NBER was, in general, recognized as an empiricism that emphasized fact gathering and the consequent discovery of empirical regularities. This empiricism was understood as a process of hypothesis seeking with minimal help from *a priori* theory. Consequently, many of the NBER's studies on business cycles focused on "faithful observation and summarizing of the cyclical characteristics of a large number of economic series" (Koopmans, 1947, p. 163). A leading example is the study of Burns and Mitchell (1946).

A dispute between the two institutions over methodology occurred when Koopmans (1947) wrote a critical review of Burns and Mitchell (1946). Vining (1949a) rebutted, defending the NBER, and both rejoined (Koopmans, 1949c; Vining, 1949b.) It was during this dispute that Vining clearly presented the NBER's criticism of the Cowles Commission's econometric approach.

According to Vining, the theoretical framework the Cowles Commission adopted is that of neoclassical economics, which adheres to the Marshallian and Walrasian tradition. The structural estimation of simultaneous equations, in particular, is a quantitative expression of the Walrasian system. The Walrasian system, however, assumes that the behavior and functioning of aggregate business fluctuations can be explained exclusively in terms of the motivated behavior of individuals, who are particles within the whole[42]; thus, it considers the individual agent to be the unit of analysis. Vining (1949a) attacks this point: The "aggregate has an existence apart from its constituent particles and behavior characteristics of its own not deducible from the behavior characteristics of the particles" (p. 79). Therefore, one "should work toward an explicit delineation of the entity itself – its structure and functioning" (p. 79). In other words:

Much of the statistical regularities that are to be observed in population phenomena and that are relevant for the discussion of economic problems involves the behavior of social organisms that are distinctly more than simple algebraic aggregates of consciously economizing individuals. . . . In a positive sense the aggregate has an existence over and above the existence of Koopmans' individual units and behavior characteristics that may not be deducible from the behavior of these component parts. (pp. 80–1)

It seems that Vining's criticism of the neoclassical framework comes from the institutionalist tradition of Veblen and Mitchell.

Another of Vining's main criticisms concerns the Neyman-Pearson type of statistical theory that had been an important statistical tool for the Cowles Commission. The Neyman-Pearson type of theory, which Haavelmo called the probability approach, emphasizes the estimation and testing of hypotheses, whereas traditional statistics deals basically with the description of the data presented, deemphasizing the estimation of properties of a population from a sample. Vining (1949a) argues that "statistical economics is too narrow in scope if it includes just the estimation of postulated relations" (p. 85). Descriptive statistics is equally important as a

---

[42] Koopmans (1949c), in his reply to Vining (1949a), conceded that "the choices of individuals are restrained by a framework of institutional rules enforced or adhered to by a government, the banking system and other institutions" (p. 87). Nonetheless, he did not fail to note that "in a deeper analysis, these rules and the changes in them would need to be explained further from choices by individuals interacting, in various degrees of association with each other, through political processes" (ibid., p. 87). That is to say, he believed that the behavior of institutions could be explained in terms of the individual optimizing agent. Today's theory of economic institutions tends to view the institution as an outcome of the optimization behavior of individual agents. See, for instance, Karaken and Wallace (1980). It is remarkable that Koopmans anticipated such an interpretation of economic institutions.

guide to understanding the nature of the phenomena at hand. In fact, the NBER's statistical method includes such processes as gathering and classifying data and discovering empirical regularities from them. Furthermore, as Haavelmo (1944) clearly points out, if the construction of the tentative theoretical model is a thought process irrelevant to the sampling theory, an accumulation of knowledge by means of descriptive statistics, like that of Burns and Mitchell (1946), would not be a worse method of seeking hypotheses than the econometric approach.

Vining's criticism, although forceful and clear, is that of a member of the opposing camp (see Ames, 1948), and thus fails to appreciate the limits and possibilities of the Cowles Commission method from its own perspective. Vining did not question whether the econometric approach could achieve its objective, that is, estimating the true structure and predicting the effect of policy. This question was addressed by Friedman and Keynes.

Skeptics of the econometric approach

It is well known that both Keynes and Friedman were skeptical of the econometric movement in the late 1930s and 1940s. Keynes's (1939, 1940) position was reflected in his famous criticism of Tinbergen (1939), and Friedman's (1939, 1951) in a review of Tinbergen (1939) and comments on Christ (1951).

Keynes's criticism of Tinbergen's pioneering work on business cycles seemed to be related to his fundamental methodological view, the roots of which go back to his *Treatise on Probability*. In the *Treatise*, Keynes regards probability as a degree of rational belief and thus rejects the cardinal measurability of probability directly suggested by the frequency theory. It follows from such a view on probability that inductive generalization by statistical inference is nearly impossible, and thus its use should be limited, especially when the generalization is related to predictions. Instead, Keynes emphasizes statistical descriptions. In another publication (Keynes, 1939), he asks essentially the same question as in the *Treatise*:

How far are these curves and equations meant to be no more than a piece of historical curve-fitting and description, and how far do they make inductive claims with reference to the future as well as the past?

Thirty years ago I used to be occupied in examining the slippery problem of passing from statistical description to inductive generalization in the case of simple correlation; and today in the era of multiple correlation I do not find that in this respect practice is much improved. (p. 566)

In order to apply the method of multiple correlation, the homogeneity of the environment through time should be assumed:

The most important condition is that the environment in all relevant respects, other than the fluctuations in those factors of which we take particular account, should be uniform and homogeneous over a period of time. We cannot be sure that such conditions will persist in the future, even if we find them in the past. (Keynes, 1939, p. 566)

Keynes's concern with a fundamental instability of economic data, in fact, had been a disturbing factor even to the proponents of the econometric approach. Tinbergen and Haavelmo were also uneasy with the issue of the autonomy of the system, and to Koopmans this problem had surfaced as the identification problem.

Consequently, to Keynes, the early econometric movement seemed unlikely to fulfill the demand for inductive generalization that would permit proving and disproving theories as well as making inferences about the future. Therefore, it was his conclusion that econometrics was of limited value. "The object of statistical study is not so much to fill in missing variables with a view to prediction, as to test the relevance and validity of the model" (Keynes, 1973, p. 296).[43] That is, statistical methods should be confined to statistical description and testing in a modest sense. Moreover, Keynes's view of econometrics seems to be consistent with his view of economics: "Economics is a science of thinking in terms of models joined to the art of choosing models which are relevant to the contemporary world. It is compelled to be this, because, unlike the typical natural science, the material to which it is applied is, in too many respects, not homogeneous through time" (Keynes, 1973, p. 296).

Along with his methodological objections to econometrics, Keynes anticipated certain technical issues that are still serious problems for today's econometric practice.[44] In this regard, Hendry (1980) provides a long list of the issues raised by Keynes: omitted-variables bias, building models with unobservable variables such as expectations, spurious correlations from the use of proxy variables and simultaneity, the multicollinearity problem, the assumption of linear functional forms, misspecifying the dynamic reactions and lag lengths, incorrectly prefiltering the data, invalidly inferring causes from correlations, and nonconstant parameters.

Whereas Keynes's criticism of econometrics is close to the view that no economic theory is testable, Friedman does not deny the importance of

[43] One should be careful not to interpret "test" in the citation as proving or disproving the model. It simply means checking the relevance of the model.

[44] It is also true that Keynes made some misinformed comments on Tinbergen (1939). For instance, he seemed to be ignorant of the theory of random summation, which had been introduced by Slutsky (1937) and Frisch (1933), believing that a linear equation could not generate oscillations. Keynes's misinformation has frequently been cited as evidence that Keynes did not have the necessary technical knowledge to understand Tinbergen's work. In spite of his technical incompetence in some aspects, however, Keynes's criticism has been widely accepted as significant. See Pheby (1985) and Hendry (1980).

testing the validity of theories. His criticism of the econometric movement is simply that the Cowles Commission method does not provide an appropriate test of theories. By investigating the prediction performances of Tinbergen's 1939 model and Klein's econometric model, he concluded that the experiments were unsuccessful. Such failure meant that it was not possible by means of the Cowles Commission method to construct a stable system of equations over time. Unlike Keynes, who understood this mainly as a limitation of the econometric method itself, Friedman considers the failures of econometric models to be telling evidence of the unsatisfactory state of our knowledge and underdevelopment of the dynamic theory:

> Our theory of relative prices is almost entirely a static theory – a theory of position, not of movement. . . . The important point is that the existing theory of relative prices does not really help to narrow appreciably the range of admissible hypotheses about the *dynamic* forces at work. (Friedman, 1951, p. 113)

More concretely, he suggests that a theory of economic change "will have to be concerned very largely with leads and lags, with intertemporal relations among phenomena, with the mechanism of transmission of impulses – precisely the kind of thing about which neither contemporary price theory nor contemporary monetary theory has much to say" (Friedman, 1951, p. 114).

However, Friedman also seems to be dissatisfied with the way the econometric method was perceived – the hope that econometrics would provide a *decisive* test of economic hypotheses. Recognizing both the tentative validity of any hypothesis not yet empirically disproved and the extreme difficulty of testing economic hypotheses, he dismisses the idea of a decisive test: "The choice among alternative hypotheses equally consistent with the available evidence must to some extent be arbitrary" (Friedman, 1953, p. 10). Then what is the appropriate role of empirical inference? To Friedman, the importance of empirical evidence lies as much in the construction of hypotheses as in the testing of their validity (see Friedman, 1953, esp. pp. 12–14). Thus, he concludes in his review of Tinbergen (1939) that "the methods used by Tinbergen do not and cannot provide an empirically tested explanation of business cycle movements. His methods are entirely appropriate, however, for deriving tentative hypotheses about the nature of cyclical behavior" (Friedman, 1939, p. 660). This view of statistical inference is consistent with that of the NBER, which emphasizes the role of hypothesis seeking.[45]

---

[45] For a plausible interpretation of Friedman's methodology, see Hirsch and de Marchi (1985). Unlike many others who have interpreted Friedman's methodology, these writers clearly distinguish Friedman's famous 1953 paper on methodology from what he is actually doing by directing their attention to inconsistencies between his methodology and practice. Completely ignoring Friedman's methodological statements, they reconstruct Friedman's methodol-

An idea shared by Keynes and Friedman is that the system of equations estimated by the econometric method tends to be unstable over time and thus fails to provide inductive generalization (Keynes) or a decisive test of business cycle theories (Friedman). Moreover, both suggest that statistical tests cannot be decisive, and thus the role of econometrics should be expanded to include not only testing but statistical description (Keynes) and hypothesis seeking (Friedman). It is remarkable that both Keynes and Friedman, two giants of twentieth-century economics, hold roughly the same methodological view.

ogy by carefully analyzing his actual works. They conclude that for Friedman statistical inferences are useful to the extent that they are helpful in hypothesis seeking and that a guide to hypothesis seeking is either economic intuition – the tradition of the Chicago school – or Dewey's pragmatism – which represents the American intellectual climate – or both.

CHAPTER 4

Hayek, the Cowles Commission, and equilibrium business cycle theory

The two preceding chapters presented some historical accounts of two central features of the equilibrium business cycle theory (EBCT): the equilibrium approach to business cycles and its econometric strategy.

In Chapter 2, the history of cycle theory was examined from a hypothetical perspective as the history of theoretical attempts to incorporate business cycles into classical equilibrium theory. Viewed in this way, business cycle theories in the nineteenth century were an apparent failure, since they endeavored to construct a new foundation of economic reasoning beyond the classical tradition, rather than revise and extend equilibrium theory. The task of either extending the realm of classical theory so as to explain the puzzling business cycle or developing a cycle theory based on classical propositions was largely left to cycle theorists of the interwar period, in particular to Hayek. Though his cycle theory was rejected by Keynesian economists and thus disconnected from what became for a time the dominant mode of economic thinking, it was a genuine theory of the cycle that fell within the strict tradition of classical doctrine.

In Chapter 3, the early econometric movement was discussed at length to provide a basis for understanding the Cowles Commission method in historical context. The econometric approach to business cycles, virtually launched by the commission, provided a completely different way of looking at the old puzzle of the cycle phenomenon. In brief, this approach showed that, once a stable economic structure was discovered by means of econometric inquiry, important characteristics of business cycles like periodicity and amplitude could be derived directly from the parameters of the econometric system. Discovering a stable econometric system was equivalent to explaining turning points in the course of cycles, as descriptive cycle theories did. The econometric approach, as well as the impact of Keynesian economics, seems in retrospect to have contributed to the sudden death of interwar business cycle theories.

A continuing problem for econometrics, however, was that of discovering a stable system. Among many different approaches to the problem, the Cowles Commission method acknowledged the need to rest on both economic theory and empirical observations. The NBER, by contrast, adopted a kind of empiricist position that completely dismissed classical equilibrium theory and relied heavily on careful empirical observations in discovering the true structure. Skeptics of the econometric movement allowed only a limited role for econometrics and emphasized the preeminence of *a priori* theory. Heated disputes over these econometric methodologies were later resolved by the Cowles Commission method.

As pointed out in Chapter 1, the EBCT is built on two tightly linked principles: the equilibrium approach to business cycles and its econometric strategy. These principles do have antecedents, however. The former was seriously dealt with by Hayek during the interwar years, and the latter parallels the Cowles Commission method. The first section of this chapter presents a historical comparison between the EBCT and Austrian cycle theory, in particular, Hayek's theory. This comparison, it is hoped, will provide a better understanding both of today's EBCT and of interwar-period cycle theory. The next section undertakes a historical examination of the problem of expectations in relation to intertemporal equilibrium analysis. In the last section it is argued that the Cowles Commission method, properly interpreted, adopts the same econometric strategy as the EBCT. In this regard, today's EBCT is just a child of the Cowles Commission method.

The EBCT and Hayek's theory of the cycle

It has often been claimed that Austrian cycle theory shares some important similarities with the EBCT.[1] Lucas (1977) argues that Hayek's theory of cycles is an intellectual precursor of the EBCT and that the EBCT has resumed the interwar-period tradition of the equilibrium approach to business cycles, which was superseded by the Keynesian revolution. Milgate (1979), Buto (1985), and Boehm (1985) claim that Hayek is one of the originators of the notion of "intertemporal equilibrium," to which "rational expectations equilibrium" is subordinate. Kantor (1979) even points out that the notion of rational expectations was not foreign to the Austrians (such as Lachman) in the interwar years, though it was not fully conceptualized.

The literature on this issue suggests that the EBCT is not a sudden invention of a few contemporary theorists and that the roots of its major

---

[1] For a full discussion of Austrian economics, see O'Driscoll and Rizzo (1985). These authors attempt to find some common ground between two seemingly incompatible currents in the interwar years, represented by Keynes and the Austrians, by reinterpreting their theories as challenges to the problem of uncertainty in the historical time plane. This could be a fresh and interesting vantage point from which to view the interwar-period theories, which have gone largely unexploited by historians of the discipline. See also O'Driscoll (1986).

arguments can be traced back to earlier economic thinking, especially the interwar-period theories. Although it is appropriate and justifiable to stress these basic themes in the literature, no systematic attempt to compare these historically distant theoretical edifices has been made. In this and the following section, the theoretical problematic of incorporating business cycles into equilibrium theory is adopted as a yardstick of comparison,[2] and Hayek's way of solving the problem is compared with the EBCT's in the hope of clarifying similarities and dissimilarities between them, and between the EBCT and Austrian theory in general.

If business cycles are to be understood within the logic of classical equilibrium theory, the starting point must be the price mechanism. That is to say, cyclical fluctuations have to be explained by, or at least shown to be not inconsistent with, the theory of relative prices; otherwise any proposed explanation of cycles cannot be said to be based on equilibrium theory. Once the working of relative prices is premised as an arbiter of cyclical fluctuations, the next step is to examine why the relative price mechanism in the real world is not working as it is presumed to work in the Walrasian equilibrium system, or how individuals' planned behaviors have unplanned consequences such as business cycles.

On this question, Hayek and the EBCT propose essentially the same theoretical idea: noisy price signals. Lucas (1977), who is credited with having introduced the EBCT into macroeconomic thinking, states his theoretical premise as follows: "Since in a competitive economy, employment and output of various kinds are chosen by agents in response to price movements, it seemed appropriate to begin by rationalizing the observed quantity movements as rational or optimal responses to observed price movements" (Lucas, 1977; 1981, p. 232).

Observed price movements, however, do not furnish to the agent all of the information necessary for him to live in the Walrasian world of certainty. Price movements do provide some critical information for the individual's optimal decision making, but price signals are "noisy"

---

[2] Lucas (1977) claims that the main theme of the interwar business cycle theories was incorporating business cycles into the system of equilibrium theory. This claim is by no means true. Even though the equilibrium approach in fact fascinated many interwar cycle theorists, there was no wide agreement among them as to the basic direction of cycle research. Mitchell's atheoretical approach, which completely discredits equilibrium theory, was in a sense more influential than the equilibrium approach. Although Lucas's interpretation of the interwar cycle theories is flatly wrong, his characterization of the EBCT as a resumption of the interwar equilibrium approach might be a useful starting point for a comparison of the two bodies of theory.

because of the fundamental nature of the capitalist economy.[3] The consequence of optimal responses to noisy price signals is deviation from the Walrasian equilibrium path, that is, cyclical fluctuations. Somewhat strikingly, business cycles are then the path unintentionally chosen by individuals in their voluntary and rational decision making.

As Lucas (1980) acknowledges, "The idea that speculative elements play a key role in business cycles, that these events seem to involve agents reacting to imperfect signals in a way which, after the fact, appears inappropriate, has . . . been a commonplace in the verbal tradition of business cycle theory at least since Mitchell" (Lucas 1980; 1981, p. 286).[4] The idea of noisy price signals is indeed a very old one (see Mitchell, 1951). It can be traced back to Sismondi and the writings of Continental cycle theorists such as Tugan-Baranovsky, Spiethoff, and Aftalion.[5] In the Continental tradition, the idea that prices do not carry all the information relevant to market clearing was a forceful theoretical weapon against Say's law, the validity of which was consistently doubted by Continental economists. Furthermore, when this idea was interwoven with a Marxist critique of capitalism, such that the market economy was seen to be structurally planless and anarchistic, it became popular enough to be a common theme of Continental cycle theory. Thus, it can be said that, in the interwar period, the idea of noisy price signals was perceived to be critical for an explanation of cycles. Hayek, who never lost contact with the Continental tradition as such, in particular clarified and elaborated the idea of noisy price signals, excising the Marxist elements around it.

Hayek, following the Austrian tradition, begins with virtually the same theoretical propositions as Lucas: that the theory of the cycle ought to be based on classical equilibrium theory; that the main component of every

---

[3] Both Lucas and Hayek hold that the source of spurious price signals is money. In the literature on real business cycles, however, real shocks like random changes in tastes and technologies tend to be emphasized as the force behind the price movement, though the idea of a monetary shock does not contradict it. The common denominator between the Lucas-type EBCT and its variant, the theory of real business cycles, is the proposition that the cycle is a consequence of individuals' optimal responses to price movements, which is called the "optimization foundation" in Chapter 1. See O'Driscoll (1977).

[4] Similarly, when Lucas (1981) states that "if Wesley Mitchell could view agents as 'signal processors' in 1913, then I saw no reason to regard my own adoption of this viewpoint in 1972 as unduly speculative" (p. 9), he seems to attribute the origin of the idea of noisy price signals to Mitchell, which is not correct. Lucas's ambiguous use of terms, not infrequent in his writings, might be responsible for this kind of misrepresentation.

[5] See Chapter 2.

explanation of cycles must be price misperception; and that money is a triggering force behind cyclical fluctuations. As for price misperception, Hayek (1944) notes that "it may be that the prices existing when [individuals] made their decisions and on which they had to base their views about the future have created expectations which must necessarily be disappointed" and that one must "distinguish between what we may call justified errors, caused by the price system, and sheer errors about the course of external events" (p. 355). The price signals perceived by individuals can be misleading and can thus fool them simultaneously and in the same direction.

The view that misleading price signals are the catalysts of cyclical fluctuations belongs to the tradition of methodological individualism, which in the context of economics means that microeconomic or individual behavior is fundamental to explanations of aggregated phenomena. That is, aggregated phenomena as cyclical fluctuations have to be understood on the level of disaggregated individual behaviors. On this account the theories of Hayek and of Lucas can be readily included in the category of methodological individualism. Because of this common factor, Lucas's EBCT is sometime called "neo-Austrian" economics (see Laidler, 1982).[6]

The fact that both theories understand the cycle to be a consequence of individuals' voluntary choice in the situation of misleading price movements is critical, because they are thus in full agreement as to the starting point of solving the problem of business cycles. In spite of this similarity, however, there exist substantial differences between Austrian cycle theory and the EBCT. These differences concern (a) market process analysis, (b) the theory of money, and (c) the theory of investment or capital.

First and probably most important, the Austrians emphasize the market process. Compared with the mutual determinism of the Walrasian general equilibrium system, process analysis focuses on the market process by which coordination is reached among the disparate plans of individuals, rather than on equilibrium states themselves. In fact, according to the Austrians, the driving force of the capitalist economy is its market process, which can be interpreted as a process of discovery under the circumstance

---

[6] For instance, "In their methodological individualism, their stress on the market mechanism as a device for disseminating information, and their insistence that the business-cycle is the central problem for macroeconomics, Robert E. Lucas, Jr., Robert J. Barro, Thomas J. Sargent, and Neil Wallace, who are the most prominent contributors to this new body of doctrine, place themselves firmly in the intellectual tradition pioneered by Ludwig von Mises and Friedrich von Hayek. Certainly their work is much more closely related to traditional 'Austrian' economics than to the 'Classical' macroeconomics of Alfred Marshall and Arthur C. Pigou" (Laidler, 1982, ix).

of fundamental uncertainty and ignorance of economic life. Therefore, a profound advantage of the price mechanism over other forms of economic institutions lies in its *process*, which involves a learning procedure toward the discovery of as yet unperceived opportunities and their exploitation, while at the same time maintaining a process of coordination among disparate individual plans. This is essentially a rekindling of Smith's invisible-hand doctrine, yet it explains a great deal, such as the Austrians' uneasiness with the deterministic Walrasian equilibrium theory,[7] their denial of mathematical and quantitative economics, and their opposition to policy intervention.

A main difference between Hayek's cycle theory and the EBCT is therefore that, in Hayek's theory, the equilibrating process or a teleological adjustment process toward the equilibrium state plays a key role, whereas in the EBCT the economy is assumed always to be in the equilibrium state.[8] In other words, according to the EBCT, the economy is in a continuum of equilibrium, instantaneously absorbing successive external shocks, whereas in Hayek's theory the market economy is in a process of moving toward equilibrium in which individuals ceaselessly learn about their environment and adjust themselves to newly perceived external shocks. In Hayek's theory of the cycle, this equilibrating process is represented by sluggish wage adjustment and consequent income adjustment, which explains the recurrence of cycles – the very same problem that confronted the Lucas-type EBCT and caused the emergence of real business cycle theories.

The second difference between Hayek's theory and the EBCT involves the theory of money. Although it is true that both Hayek and Lucas find in money "the force triggering the real business cycle" (Lucas, 1977; 1981, p. 233), they differ with respect to *how*. Hayek objects to the doctrine of the quantity theory. He claims that monetary theory lags behind the development of economics in general. Thus, we err

. . . if we try to establish *direct* causal connections between the *total* quantity of money, the *general level* of all prices and, perhaps, also the *total* amount of production. For none of these magnitudes *as such* ever exerts an influence on the decisions of individuals; yet it is on the assumption of a knowledge of the decisions of individuals that the main propositions of non-monetary economic theory are based. (Hayek, 1935, p. 3)

That is, "neither aggregates nor averages do act upon one another, and it

[7] In fact, contemporary Austrian economists are highly critical of the New Classical economics, and most of their criticism is directed at its conceptualization of equilibrium as an exact mutual determination. See O'Driscoll and Rizzo (1985).

[8] Because of Hayek's adoption of an equilibrating process, his cycle theory is sometimes labeled a disequilibrium theory. For instance, Hansen (1951) classifies Hayek's theory as a disequilibrium overinvestment theory.

will never be possible to establish necessary connections of cause and effect between them as we can between individual phenomena, individual prices, etc." (Hayek, 1935, pp. 3–4). This objection to the quantity theory, of course, reflects the Austrian spirit of methodological individualism. On the other hand, Lucas and the New Classical economists adhere to the doctrine of the neutrality of money, a version of the quantity theory that claims that money is neutral as far as its movement is perceived by individuals.[9] In the EBCT, aggregates, like the quantity of money, are necessary information for individuals in their decision making, since their movement contains information about relative prices. To Hayek, however, individuals are incapable of observing the quantity of money, and it is even irrelevant to them. Because the economy is assumed to be in an equilibrating process, not in the equilibrium state, they cannot extract from monetary movement any useful information about the relative price movement. Instead of such a quantity theory, Hayek, following Mises, suggests a monetary theory in which the individual's income transmits the effect of monetary movements to his decision making – the Cantillon effect.

A final difference between the two cycle theories can be found in their theory of capital. In the EBCT, all individual agents are assumed to be alike. From the perspective of a representative agent, investment is nothing but the leftovers after consumption, and thus he can solve simultaneously the problem of investment and consumption. When such an individual's decision is aggregated, it becomes the EBCT's investment theory (see Lucas and Prescott, 1971), which is therefore little different from its consumption theory based on the representative agent's optimizing behavior. In contrast, Hayek distinguishes different kinds of individuals, such as consumers and investors, and emphasizes such relationships between them as coordination failures.[10] At the same time, this assumption of different

---

[9] It is somewhat paradoxical that, in spite of the fact that the EBCT has grown up on the foundation of monetarism, which emphasizes the importance of money, theories of the real business cycle deemphasize money, and the reason for their relative neglect of money can also be found in monetarists' adherence to the neutral money doctrine.

[10] In a sense Hayek's theory of the cycle can be said to be built around the conception of coordination failure, which comes from the tradition of Continental cycle theory, even though Hayek completely succeeds in explaining by the logic of the price mechanism this coordination failure between consumption goods and investment goods. The coordination failure, also referred to as horizontal or vertical maladjustment or as disproportionality, has been a major theme of Continental cycle theory. It simply means the mismatch between resources and wants across different sectors. Recently some theories of the real

kinds of agents opens the possibility of developing a capital theory that is independent of consumption theory.

The similarities and dissimilarities between Hayek and the EBCT seem to reflect their different intellectual roots. As noted, Hayek's theory and Austrian cycle theory are centered around methodological individualism and market process analysis, whereas the EBCT strictly follows the optimization foundation as a theoretical heuristic, which is related to the Fisherine tradition peculiar to American economics. As Tobin (1985) points out, "Fisher's methodologies, not just his use of mathematics but his explicit formulations of problems as constrained optimizations, [are] the accepted style of present-day theorizing" (p. 34). The Fisherine style of theorizing has been dominant in American macroeconomics, from the emphasis in the 1950s and 1960s on constructing the aggregate investment function and consumption function on an optimization foundation, to the contemporary EBCT.

Expectations and equilibrium

In the discussion of interwar-period cycle theories presented in Chapter 2, it was noted that the efforts to incorporate cycle phenomena into equilibrium theory took two forms: an attempt to explain cycle phenomena directly by the logic of the price mechanism and a reformation of the existing classical equilibrium theory as a more rigorous and extended one. The latter stemmed from a widespread recognition among interwar theorists that, whereas the real world exemplified by cycle phenomena is essentially dynamic, equilibrium theory is static and timeless. This recognition naturally led to a reexamination of the concept of equilibrium, both its assumptions and its dynamic nature. As Hayek (1944) pointed out, "There can be no doubt that here some of the formulations of the theory of equilibrium prove to be of little use and that not only their particular content but also the idea of equilibrium as such which they use will require a certain amount of revision" (p. 352).

When the time element is introduced into equilibrium analysis, that is, when the static theory is extended so as to be dynamic, the conception of the state of equilibrium has to be revised: It must be described as a continuum of equilibria – as an intertemporal equilibrium. Two problems arise, however: first, the role of the price system in a dynamic setting, and second, the conditions or assumptions necessary for such a dynamic equilibrium.

business cycle have revived the idea of coordination failure among sectors. For instance, Black (1981, 1982) claims that adjustment costs prevent a smooth coordination among sectors and this causes cyclical fluctuations.

The static equilibrium theory is concerned largely with the reallocation of resources through the price system at one point in time. In the space and time plane, however, the price system functions to allocate goods between different points in time. Thus, the price of a good at present implicitly reflects the intertemporal exchange for the same good in the future. In other words, differences in prices of technically equivalent goods at various moments in time reflect differences in the conditions of tastes and technologies at different points in time "in just the same way as such goods will not carry the same price if they are located at different places" (Hayek, 1984, p. 76). There are fundamental difficulties in transferring goods from one point in time to another, and because of these barriers the relative prices between different points in time, the intertemporal exchange rate, clearly reflect the individual's subjective intertemporal evaluations of given goods. For example, the interest rate can be interpreted as the price of giving up today's spending for tomorrow's spending (Fisher's "time impatience"; Fisher, 1930). Or the interest rate's function of maintaining "equilibrium between production for the future and that for the present" (Hayek, 1984, p. 111) can be emphasized, as in a Böhm-Bawerkian theory of interest. At any rate, the conception of intertemporal equilibrium definitely allows one to view the price system differently and to clarify some other roles of the system that had heretofore been poorly understood. Hayek's later studies on knowledge and society, in which the price mechanism is portrayed as an efficient allocator of information, would be additional examples of such an exploration of the extended nature of the price system.

Identifying the necessary assumptions for the intertemporal equilibrium raises another group of questions. Hayek (1944) sketches the assumptions as follows:

It has become clear that, instead of completely disregarding the time element, we must make very definite assumptions about the attitude of persons towards the future. The assumptions of this kind which are implied in the concept of equilibrium are essentially that everybody foresees the future correctly and that this foresight includes not only the changes in the objective data but also the behavior of all the other people with whom he expects to perform economic transactions. (p. 353)

Thus, the assumption is that of correct foresight with respect to both the external data and the behaviors of others, that is, the workings of the economic system itself.[11] More precisely, in the state of equilibrium, "the external data correspond to the common expectations of all the members of

---

[11] Hutchison (1937) distinguishes between perfect expectations and correct expectations. By perfect expectations he means omniscience about the future, and by correct expectations, simply that the particular plan adopted by an individ-

the society," and "compatibility exists between the different plans which the individuals composing it have made for action in time" (Hayek, 1937, p. 41).

The rational expectations hypothesis would correspond to assuming both the mathematical expectations of the external data and complete knowledge about the workings of the economic system.[12] The rational expectations hypothesis postulates that an individual's expectations of future events are identical with the mathematical expectations conditional on the given information set, which includes complete knowledge about the economic system as well as knowledge about past external events. Therefore, if either of these assumptions is not satisfied, the hypothesis does not hold. If the assumption of complete knowledge about the economic system cannot be maintained, as in the case of imperfect competition, then the situation comes to be the case of Morgenstern's (1976) paradox:

Sherlock Holmes, pursued by his opponent, Moriarity, leaves London for Dover. The train stops at a station on the way, and he alights there rather than travelling on to Dover. He has seen Moriarity at the railway station, recognizes that he is very clever and expects that Moriarity will take a faster special train in order to catch him in Dover. Holmes' anticipation turns out to be correct. But what if Moriarity had been still more clever, had estimated Holmes' mental abilities better and had foreseen his actions accordingly? Then, obviously, he would have travelled to the

ual turns out to be undisappointed, though he does not foresee all the consequences of his alternatives. Despite Hutchison's distinction it seems that the interwar theorists did not pay much attention to it and used the terms interchangeably. Hayek was no exception.

[12] As is widely known, Muth (1961) is credited with having formulated the rational expectations hypothesis. However, the concept of rational expectations is not totally new; the possibility of such a concept was discussed by interwar theorists. Although somewhat vague and unsystematic, Tintner (1938) distinguishes between two types of errors in economic behavior. The first type is "defined as a deviation from the rational behavior which yields maximum utility"; errors of this type would be rather small and thus independently and normally distributed. "Errors of the second kind, however, are likely to be widespread and approximately the same in all branches of industry" (Tintner, 1938, pp. 145–6), and thus they are systematic errors that are serially correlated. Here the errors of the first type seem to correspond to unsystematic errors in the rational expectations hypothesis. Tintner, after distinguishing two types of errors, speculates that "the random part of economic time series . . . appears to be probably a result of errors of the first kind" (p. 147) and that errors of the second type are responsible for the shape of economic time series. Tintner's interpretation of time series is surprisingly close to that of the EBCT. It is likely that the mathematical statisticians in the 1930s at least saw the possibility of formulating the rational expectations hypothesis, although they did not fully recognize its significance.

intermediate station. Holmes, again, would have had to calculate that, and he himself would have decided to go on to Dover. Whereupon, Moriarity would again have "reacted" differently. Because of so much thinking they might not have been able to act at all or the intellectually weaker of the two would have surrendered to the other in the Victoria Station, since the whole fight would have become unnecessary. Examples of this kind can be drawn from everywhere. (pp. 173–4)

Given the fact that "a calculation of the effects of one's own future behavior always rests on the expected future behavior of others and *vice versa*" (Tintner, 1938, p. 173), Morgenstern's paradox shows that there can be no resolution that simultaneously satisfies the expectations of all individuals concerned. Simply put, "Unlimited foresight and economic equilibrium are thus irreconcilable with one another" (p. 174). The trick of this paradox, however, lies in its presupposition that an individual's future behavior influences the behavior of others. Thus, under the condition of perfect competition in which no one can influence anybody, one can escape Morgenstern's paradox. "Perfect expectation is only compatible with 'competitive' conditions, that is conditions where no one person's conduct can affect the conduct, and the result of the calculations on which it is based, of another" (Hutchinson, 1937, p. 644).

Therefore, when the condition of perfect competition is violated, regardless of rational expectations or perfect foresight, as in the case of monopolistic competition and duopoly, Morgenstern's paradox surfaces and there cannot be any determination of equilibrium. This is the situation that Sargent (1984) calls "the internal contradiction of the rational expectations econometrics"[13]:

Suppose that the free parameters of private agents' preferences and constraints have been estimated during an estimation period, and then are used to calculate a new and improved strategy for government policy in the future. On the one hand, if this procedure were in fact likely to be persuasive in having the policy recommendation actually adopted soon, it would mean that the original econometric model with its arbitrarily specified rules for government policy had been misspecified. A rational expectations model during the estimation period ought to reflect the procedure by which policy is thought later to be influenced, for agents are posited to be speculating about government decisions into infinite future. On the other hand, if this procedure is not thought likely to be a source of persuasive policy recommendations, most of its appeal vanishes. (pp. 412–13)

That is, if government policy is believed to have room for improvement, the Holmes–Moriarity story becomes real and, without exception, any rational expectations model always misspecifies the economic structure. If, however, policy is supposed always to be optimum, Morgenstern's paradox

---

[13] In a similar context, Kydland and Prescott (1977) discuss the "time-inconsistency" problem of optimal policy; their insights are essentially the same as those of Sargent and Morgenstern.

is solvable. But then what is policy analysis, and, more broadly, economics in general, for? Morgenstern's paradox, which clearly shows a serious contradiction inherent in the study of equilibrium and expectations, is resurfacing in the New Classical economics as one of the philosophical difficulties concerning the nature of government policy.

Cowles Commission method revisited

Part of the importance of the Cowles Commission method in the history of business cycle theory is that it provided an alternative to the then-standard verbal discussions of business cycles. Although the impact of the Keynesian revolution in part explains the sudden disappearance of interwar cycle theories in the postwar years, historical hindsight suggests that the Cowles Commission method, the econometric approach to business cycles, was also partially responsible for this discontinuity. Why this is so becomes clear once the Cowles Commission method is understood.

A fundamental idea of the econometric approach is that of distinguishing external shocks from the propagation mechanism, an idea established by Slutsky, Yule, and Frisch.[14] From this perspective, cyclical fluctuations in economic time series are an outcome of continual external shocks to the propagation mechanism. In other words, when continual shocks hit the economic system, the system absorbs and propagates the shocks in such a way that their consequences exhibit cyclical features. An immediate implication of this idea is that cycle research should concentrate on the explanation of the propagation mechanism, without bothering with the superficial characteristics of cycles, such as their upper and lower turning points. Because the statistical characteristic of the propagation mechanism in the absence of external shocks is damped oscillation, which can be represented by a system of low-order difference equations, if such a system is statistically identified, then observed cyclical movements can be explained in a straightforward way. Therefore, the focus of conventional business cycle theories on turning points and periodicity is less important than the statistical identification of a stable system. This shift in emphasis seems to be one of the theoretical reasons for the interruption of the pursuit of descriptive interwar cycle theories.

The construction of a stable structure that would generate cycles, however, was not an easy task. The early researchers of the Cowles Commission, Marschak, Haavelmo, and Koopmans, opted for a methodological position emphasizing the role of both economic theory and

---

[14] See the second and third sections of Chapter 3 on the empirical and econometric approaches to the business cycle, respectively.

empirical observation. In explaining the identification problem, Koopmans (1949b) states that

statistical inference unsupported by economic theory applies to whatever statistical regularities and stable relationships can be discerned in the data. Such purely empirical relationships when discernible are likely to be due to the presence and peristence of the underlying structural relationships, and (if so) could be deduced from a knowledge of the latter. However, the direction of this deduction cannot be reversed – from the empirical to the structural relationships – except possibly with the help of a theory which specifies the form of the structural relationships. . . . The more detailed these specifications are made in the model, the greater scope is thereby given to statistical inference from the data to the structural equations. (p. 126)

So in the construction of an econometric system one foundation stone consists of the statistical tools necessary for drawing inferences from the data, and another is economic theory. More specifically, the Cowles Commission's indispensable instrument for statistical inference is the structural-equations estimation method, and the identification problem is the conceptual device that sets limits on statistical inference and channels support from economic theory. Through the process of identification, derived theoretical restrictions can be imposed to facilitate statistical inference from the data; and by testing these theoretical restrictions, economic theory acquires the opportunity to confront the facts.

As for the choice among economic theories, however, the Cowles Commission was somewhat ambiguous. Its early founders, like Koopmans and Haavelmo, seemed to favor classical equilibrium price theory as an indispensable element of the formulation of structural equations, for to them economic theory should be based on "knowledge of the motives and habit of consumers and of the profit-making objectives of business enterprise, . . . briefly, a more or less systematized knowledge of man's behavior and its motives" (Koopmans, 1947, p. 166). That is, the theoretical foundation of the econometric system had to be sought from *a priori* theory of the optimizing behavior of individuals. But contrary to their intention, most empirical works that employed the Cowles Commission method embodied very little of such theory. Klein's macroeconomic models were basically rooted in Keynesian economics. Most model builders in the spirit of the Cowles Commission simply dismissed this problem by assuming that their Keynesian behavioral equations were somehow derived from the optimization behavior of individuals. The discrepancy between the judgment of the commission's founders and the commission's econometric practice is another facet of the microfoundation problem of Keynesian macroeconomics in the 1950s and 1960s, which is reflected in abuses of ad hoc theoretical restrictions in econometric modeling.

The Cowles Commission method, compared with the EBCT's econometric strategy, can be appraised as a theoretical ancestor of the latter. Sargent clearly states:

Rational expectations macroeconomics is the logical, continuous consequence of what people like Koopmans and Hurwicz and other people, who founded the econometric techniques underlying Keynesian models, had in mind. The same philosophical desiderata for a model that those guys had in mind are what we have in mind. Koopmans and Hurwicz, very early on, said that you want to build on models based on optimizing behavior. (Klamer, 1984, p. 66)

Tobin places them in the same category of econometric strategy: "[New Classical macroeconometrics] is not different from the spirit of the Cowles Commission econometrics 40 years ago. Koopmans, Habelman [sic], and their colleagues, they too had the idea that you should use methods of econometrics which are consistent with the way in which you model the generation of the data and the error terms" (Klamer, 1984, pp. 107–8). As these contemporary authorities acknowledge, the EBCT and the Cowles Commission take the same stand on econometric strategy. Both accept Frisch's idea of distinguishing the propagation mechanism from external shocks. Both accept that economic theory is critical to or dictates statistical inferences, being skeptical of a purely empirical approach. And both accept that the kind of economic theory on which the econometric system is based has to encompass the optimizing behavior of individuals.

It can be said, therefore, that the EBCT's econometric strategy is a successor of the Cowles Commission method and has elaborated its statistical techniques and conceptions. For instance, the Cowles Commission members were not clear about the matter of structure – a central question in the history of econometrics. Haavelmo (1944), emphasizing the relative nature of the stability of structure, thought of the construction of a stable structure as a "matter of intuition and factual knowledge; it is an art" (p. 29), thereby denying the possibility of arriving at true structure through the construction of an econometric system. Though he clearly distinguished a stable econometric system from true structure, he failed to offer any conceptual criterion for judging the relative stability of the econometric system. Koopmans was not far from Haavelmo on this issue. Owing mainly to his recognition of the impossibility of discovering an absolutely stable structure, he sometimes suggested as the criterion of stability the forecasting power of the econometric system concerned and at other times the invariance of the system with respect to changes in policy (Koopmans and Barsch, 1959). In contrast to the Cowles Commission's conceptual uncertainty about the structure, according to the EBCT's econometric strategy the econometric system is structural if its behavioral equations are closely restricted to the deep parameters of such state variables as tastes, technology, and policy (see Lucas and Sargent, 1981, esp. Chap. 1). In other words cross-equation restrictions are the safeguard against changes in state variables. Lucas's critique of policy evaluation is a corollary of this definition of structure.

Another achievement of the New Classical econometrics in line with the Cowles Commission method was the construct of error terms in econometric models as forecast errors. Although Haavelmo explicitly pointed out the need for reformulating economic theory in stochastic terms, the Cowles Commission failed to provide such a theory. Thus, the EBCT's formulation of macroeconometric models in terms of dynamic optimization under rational expectations can be considered a way of resolving the Cowles Commission's dilemma.

Throughout this book, the EBCT has been examined in historical context. First, the EBCT was located in the history of business cycle theory, and then its econometric strategy was historically compared with the econometric ideas that preceded it. These historical discussions suggest both that the EBCT is not exactly the type of cycle theory that interwar cycle theorists had in mind when they talked about the incorporation of the business cycle into equilibrium theory, since these theorists never thought of the business cycle as an equilibrium phenomenon, and also that the EBCT's econometric strategy is just a child of the Cowles Commission method. However, what differentiates the EBCT categorically from its historical predecessors is its firm adherence to the optimization foundation.

Because of this foundation, the EBCT is no richer in theoretical content than were interwar cycle theories. Even though the optimization foundation enables the EBCT to resolve the microfoundation problem, it also compels a simplification of the EBCT, so that the theory of money is reduced to a simple quantity theory, the theory of capital is virtually nonexistent, and the conception of disequilibrium is simply discredited. Again, because of the optimization foundation, the EBCT is able to clarify the concept of econometric structure, which was unclear to the Cowles Commission. However, the EBCT's claim that theoretical restrictions in econometric modeling must be derived from individuals' optimizing behavior seriously restricts the boundary of econometric modeling, mainly for computational reasons and because of a lack of appropriate methods of statistical estimation. Thus, the EBCT's econometric strategy is an extreme version of the Cowles Commission method, and this makes the old criticisms of the latter still relevant to today's EBCT.

CHAPTER 5

Contemporary trends in macroeconometrics

In Chapter 4, it was suggested that the EBCT's econometric strategy is a child of the Cowles Commission method, since the EBCT shares with the latter essentially the same econometric methodology, which explicitly admits the role of *a priori* economic theory in statistical inferences from data. But what differentiates the EBCT from its historical precedecessor is its firm adherence to the optimization foundation. Although Haavelmo and Koopmans preferred equilibrium theory as the basis for the construction of an econometric system, in which the individual's optimizing behavior is assumed to provide basic explanations of economic phenomena, the Cowles Commission as a whole was not clear about how to implement this theory in actual empirical work. It might be said that the EBCT's econometric strategy, the hallmark of which is the use of cross-equation restrictions directly derived from the setting of dynamic optimization, is one possible solution to this problem.

The EBCT, like its forerunner, is not immune to criticism, some of which is discussed in this chapter. However, the criticisms that have been leveled against it also represent important alternatives to the EBCT in the contemporary scene. Not surprisingly, it will be seen that the current dispute about econometric methodology is a revival of the old methodological controversies that existed early in the econometric movement. The first section of this chapter presents an expository formulation of the EBCT's econometric strategy. In the second section, Sims's criticism of and his alternative methodological position to the EBCT are discussed. The final section deals with Hendry's econometric methodology, which, though sound and plausible, is not very familiar to American econometricians.

The EBCT's econometric strategy

When Lucas (1976) launched his critique of econometric policy evaluation, its implications were very destructive, since he claimed that none of the current macroeconometric models could provide correct comparisons of the effects of alternative policies and thus the usefulness of these models in policy analysis was highly questionable. Such a formidable threat to the existing practice of econometric modeling however, was based on relatively simple reasoning. Lucas (1976) presents his idea in a single syllogism:

[G]iven that the structure of an econometric model consists of optimal decision rules of economic agents, and that optimal decision rules vary systematically with changes in the structure of series relevant to the decision maker, it follows that any change in policy will systematically alter the structure of econometric models. (p. 41)

Put differently and somewhat more clearly, when there occurs a change in policy that is relevant to agents' decision making, agents respond by revising their optimal decisions. Consequently, the structure of the econometric model, the behavioral equations of which are simple aggregates of the agents' optimal decision rules, would be changed accordingly. Therefore, the econometric structure, which is estimated under the old policy regime, becomes invalid under the new regime and cannot be used to forecast the consequence of new policy. Agents revise their decision rules under the new regime, and this induces changes in the coefficients of the old structure.

Granted that the conventional practice of large-scale macroeconometric modeling is in principle of no use for the purpose of policy evaluation, the next question is, What would constitute a correct econometric strategy – one that is immune to the Lucas critique? Hansen and Sargent (1980) set forth the direction of such a strategy as follows:

The implication of Lucas's observation is that instead of estimating the parameters of decision rules, what should be estimated are the parameters of agents' objective functions and of the random process that they faced historically. Disentangling the parameters governing the stochastic processes that agents face from the parameters of their objective functions would enable the econometricians to predict how agents' decision rules would change across alternations in their stochastic environment. Accomplishing this task is an absolute prerequisite of reliable econometric policy evaluation. (pp. 91–92)

The execution of such an econometric strategy necessarily involves cross-equation restrictions that connect the parameters of decision rules with the deep parameters of tastes, technologies, and other stochastic environments. These restrictions allow one to predict systematically the effects of a change in policy on the coefficients in behavioral equations in an econometric model. On the one hand, constructing the econometric model on the basis of cross-equation restrictions is a safeguard against the Lucas critique. On the other, it represents a resolution of the old problem in the history of econometrics of discovering or constructing a stable econometric system, since the econometric model, constructed in this way, should be stable with respect to changes in policy and environments.

Despite its theoretical appeal, however, the EBCT's strategy is extremely difficult to carry out successfully in actual econometric practice.[1] "In applications substantial technical problems exist even about the best way of expressing these restrictions mathematically" (Hansen and Sargent, 1980, p. 92). The estimation of models subject to cross-equation restrictions is another, even more important difficulty owing to the highly nonlinear nature of these restrictions.

Partly because of these difficulties and partly because of the antipathy to large-scale Keynesian models, the early econometric work that followed the EBCT's strategy employed small-size macroeconometric models in which behavioral equations were not explicitly derived from, but were simply assumed as the consequence of, individuals' optimization. Barro (1977, 1978) has obtained some empirical results that support the rational expectations hypothesis and neutrality-of-money proposition.[2] His procedure is basically one of decomposing money growth rates into anticipated and unanticipated components; he then demonstrates that unemployment is closely related to unanticipated components and that an addition of anticipated components into the regression does not significantly improve the explanatory power. Barro's crucial auxiliary hypothesis, however, is that a certain government spending variable affects money growth rates but has no direct effect on unemployment. This assumption enables him to distinguish between anticipated and unanticipated money growth by regressing money growth rates on the set of variables that contains a government spending variable. Thus, Barro's statistical tests are tests of joint hypotheses of this assumption and the rational expectations' policy-ineffectiveness proposition, and because of this the tests cannot be regarded as definitive.

The criticism that Barro's auxiliary assumption is arbitrary reminds one of Sargent's (1976b) "observational equivalence" argument, in that Sargent claims that, since one cannot distinguish between two reduced forms of New Classical and Keynesian models, one has to introduce additional *a priori* information, that is, cross-equation restrictions, to differentiate the models.[3] What is lacking in Barro's procedure is therefore

[1] For discussions of the theoretical and technical difficulties of executing the EBCT's strategy, see Sargent (1981), Hansen and Sargent (1980, 1981), and Mishkin (1983a).

[2] See also Sargent (1976a) for the claim that empirical evidence supports the neutrality proposition, though not decisively.

[3] As Sargent (1976b) acknowledges, his claim is analogous to the Cowles Commission's contention that reduced forms are not suitable for policy evaluation. Since certain kinds of policies, like taxation on income, might change some coefficients

an explicit adaptation of cross-equation restrictions. Instead, his method relies on arbitrary assumptions that are not necessarily attributable to New Classical macroeconomics.

Given that small macroeconomic models without explicit derivation of the cross-equation restrictions from individuals' optimization have to rely on some arbitrary assumptions, it becomes clear that the correct strategy to pursue is the derivation of such cross-equation restrictions and the development of appropriate estimation methods, even though the computational techniques and statistical theory involved are extremely difficult. Specifically, the strategy includes (a) setting up an agent's dynamic optimization problem in that the agent chooses a contingency plan to maximize his expected present value,[4] (b) solving this optimization problem to derive stochastic Euler equations, (c) deriving the decision rule by eliminating the expectations operators in the Euler equations, and (d) estimating the decision rule. Although the algorithms for deriving the decision rule from the dynamic optimization setup are difficult to work with, the foremost difficulty lies in estimating the decision rule so derived. By virtue of the highly nonlinear nature of the cross-equation restrictions, and because the maximum likelihood estimator requires an exact specification of error structure, which cannot be provided without auxiliary assumptions, the usual method of maximum likelihood cannot be directly applied. Furthermore, the computational burden of evaluating the log-likelihood function requires some alternative estimation procedures like approximating the likelihood function (Hansen and Sargent, 1980) or the generalized method of moments, (GMM).[5] In particular, the GMM estimator, which was initially developed in association with the instrumental variables estimator, turns out to be a natural partner of the EBCT's econometric strategy, since dynamic rational expectations econometric models typically involve a set of orthogonality conditions (e.g., stochastic Euler equations), and one can simply estimate the parameters by choosing a single parameter that satisfies most closely these orthogonality conditions in the sample space. Considering its computational compactness and natural theoretical interpretation, the GMM estimator seems to be a

in the structural model, it is impossible to forecast policy effects without estimating the whole structure.

[4] The agent's objective function is usually expressed in quadratic form, partly because this ensures that the derived decision rule will be linear and partly because computational limitation does not allow one to adopt a more general form of objective function. Thus, quadratic objective functions are adopted in the literature not for economic reasons, but for the sake of convenience.

[5] For a discussion of the GMM estimator, see Hansen (1982), Hansen and Sargent (1982), and Hansen and Singleton (1982).

legitimate estimation method in the EBCT's econometric strategy, although its statistical properties, such as small sample properties and test statistics, are not yet fully developed.

Sims's atheoretical approach

Among the criticisms of the EBCT's econometric strategy, Sims's is one of the most influential. Not only is he skeptical of the practical applicability of the strategy, but he suggests an alternative econometric methodology. Like the Cowles Commission method, the EBCT's strategy presupposes that *a priori* theory is a prerequisite of statistical inference. Sims (1982b), in contrast, believes that theoretical restrictions in statistical inference should be kept to a minimum:

The notion that good empirical work must involve confronting the data with a model which allows the data to answer only a narrow range of questions, i.e., with a heavily restricted model, is quite incorrect. . . . It can be argued that the most influential empirical work in economics has historically been quite "unstructured", asking the data relatively vaguely specified classes of questions and leaving it to tell the story of such regularities as were actually present. (p. 333)

Accordingly, econometric models must be loosely constructed so as to leave room for the data to unfold the story. This class of loosely restricted models includes reduced forms of simultaneous-equation models and the vector autoregression (VAR) model. An apparent advantage of loosely restricted models over such heavily restricted models as the Cowles Commission's simultaneous-equation model and the rational expectations macroeconometric model is that the former do not have to deal with the complicated problem of identifying the econometric system but are at the same time capable of projecting the effects of policy.

Along with this profound methodological disagreement with the EBCT's strategy, Sims doubts its practical usefulness for the purpose of policy evaluation. According to him, the positive program of rational expectations econometrics takes insufficient account of policy endogeneity, as in conventional large-scale econometric modeling. Whereas the usual econometric analysis treats the policy variable as strictly exogenous, statistical tests like the Granger-Sims causality test do not support this specification.[6] Moreover, there are many other theoretical reasons for doubting policy exogeneity. Policies are in many cases passive reflections of real economic activity. For example, the "inside money" idea proposed by King and Plosser (1984), which claims that an increase in output induces credit expansion and thus that monetary movements are endogenous, challenges

---

[6] See Sims (1972, 1977) for the method of the causality test and Sims (1980b, 1983) for its practical application.

the usual assumption of exogeneity of monetary policy. The econometric consequences of erroneously assuming policy exogeneity would be a misspecification of the model and incorrect policy analysis.

Sims (1982a) furthermore argues that it is a mistake to think that "a policy setting is a complete set of contingency plans for the future course of policy and one chooses among such settings to achieve the best outcome" (p. 109). In practice normal policy making can hardly be described as such a once-for-all analysis and decision or policy regime shifts. "Policymakers ordinarily consider what actions to take in the next few quarters or years, reconsider their plans every few months, and repeatedly use econometric models to project the likely effects of alternative actions" (p. 109). Therefore, if policy choice is better described by continuous revisions of plans and econometric projections for the near future than by a once-for-all choice, the exact identification of an econometric system is unnecessary, since crude approximations are good enough for such limited purposes. Lucas's critique of policy evaluation thus is "a cautionary footnote to [policy] analysis rather than a deep objection to its foundations" (p. 108) – all the more so if one considers, as do Sargent (1984) and Kydland and Prescott (1977), that shifts in the expectational mechanism make it impossible to formulate an optimal contingency plan. In short, "the positive program of rational expectations econometrics . . . reproduces the main faults of standard econometric policy evaluation in exaggerated form" (Sims, 1982b, p. 334).

From this perspective, an alternative to the economic strategy of the EBCT would be an atheoretical approach to econometric policy evaluation. That is, when the exact identification of the econometric model is no longer considered to be a necessary procedure in policy analysis, one is freed from the burden of deriving identifying restrictions, a burden that has weighed heavily on both the Cowles Commission method and EBCT's econometric strategy. Loosely restricted models can serve equally well for the purpose of policy analysis.

The VAR system is a statistical device developed in this context primarily by Sims and his co-workers.[7] The VAR system is a kind of modern time-series method in which a vector of variables is regressed on its own past values. In this model, such theoretical restrictions as zero restrictions on the coefficients and cross-equation restrictions are not imposed on the coefficient matrices, so that guidance by theory is limited

---

[7] For discussions of the VAR method, see Sargent and Sims (1977), Sims (1980a) and Litterman (1980, 1984). Cooley and LeRoy (1985) offer a critique of the atheoretical approach, discussing such conceptual issues as structure, causality, and exogeneity. See also Gordon and King (1982).

only to the selection of the variables to enter into the model and the lag length. In Sims's (1980a) paper, the variables included are money, GNP, the unemployment rate, the wage rate, the price level, and the import price index, and the lag length is four quarters. Thus, the coefficient matrices are composed of four six-by-six matrices. The coefficients estimated, however, have no immediate economic meaning, although the VAR model itself can be interpreted as a reduced form of a loosely restricted structural model.[8]

Some important techniques associated with the VAR model are as follows:

1. The Granger–Sims causality test (Granger, 1969; Sims, 1972). Suppose there are two time series M and Y. According to Granger (1969), the series Y fails to Granger-cause M if, in a regression of M on lagged M and lagged Y, the latter has zero coefficients. Equivalently, according to Sims (1977), Y fails to Granger-cause M if, in a regression of Y on lagged Y and future M, the latter has zero coefficients. Furthermore, if Y fails to Granger-cause M, then M is said to be *exogenous* with respect to Y. If in addition M Granger-causes Y, then M is said to be *causally prior* to Y.

2. Innovation accounting.[9] The VAR system can be inverted under weak conditions on the coefficient matrices and written in moving-average form. From this moving-average representation, the variance of each variable in a VAR system can be decomposed into the variances of variables included, by conversion of the coefficient matrices into lower-triangular matrices. Innovation accounting summarizes the main channels of influence in the system, in that the proportion of each variable's total variance is attributed to each of the variances of variables in the system. Innovation accounting, however, has a serious defect in that the result is not invariant under changes in the ordering of the variables included. Careful investigation of the causal ordering of the variables, therefore, is a prerequisite of innovation accounting analysis.

3. Impulse response analysis. In the moving-average representation of the VAR system, each variable is a function of the orthogonalized innovations in the system, so that the response of a variable at date $t + s$ to the innovation in another variable at date t can be easily figured out. A

---

[8] In this regard Sargent (1984) suggests a different interpretation of the VAR system, in that the model is a reduced form of a system, each equation of which is derived from individuals' optimization. Sargent's interpretation amounts to imposing full theoretical restrictions on the coefficients in the VAR model, which is directly opposite to Sims's methodological position.

[9] See Sims (1980a, b) for explanations and examples of innovation accounting and impulse response analysis.

tabulation of such responses for all positive s is an impulse response function, which describes the system's response to a shock.

These techniques would be used in hypothesis seeking, forecasting,[10] and, eventually, policy analysis; impulse response analysis is particularly applicable to the latter two areas. All three provide a descriptive guide to the formulation of good theoretical models. Causality tests, for example, can be used to generate stylized facts about the causal orderings of macroeconomic variables. Then several hypotheses can be tried out to explain these facts.[11]

It can be easily discerned from the above discussion that Sims's approach concentrates on forecasting, to the relative neglect of hypothesis testing, which has been one of the important purposes of empirical research at least since the Cowles Commission. Sims's emphasis on forecasting is closely related to his methodological position. According to Sims's definition of structure, "a structural model is one which remains invariant under some specified class of hypothetical interventions, and hence is useful in predicting the effects of such intervention." Furthermore, "whether a model is structural depends on the use to which it is to be put – on what class of interventions is being considered" (Sims, 1982a, p. 332). Two observations follow from this definition of structure.

First, this relativistic definition is very similar to that of Haavelmo. Haavelmo understood structure as a matter of relative stability in an econometric model and denied the possibility of arriving at the one true system. Haavelmo's definition was succeeded by that of the Cowles Commission, and econometricians following the Cowles Commission method had difficulty defining the relative nature of structure. Although they did know that an econometric model could not be absolutely structural, they were beset by the question "structural with respect to what?" This lack of an explicit definition of structure seems to have contributed to the uncharacteristic expansion of model size in the 1950s and 1960s. In contrast, today's New Classical econometricians *believe* that the true system is composed of such state variables as taste, technology, and policy, so that a

---

[10] Sims and his co-workers have experimented with various ways of introducing Bayesian concepts into the VAR system. For example, Doan, Litterman, and Sims (1984) demonstrate a forecasting procedure in which the priors related to the model specification are selected on the ground of within-sample forecasting performance and then these priors are used to produce out-of-sample forecasts.

[11] An example of this pattern of theorizing is Litterman and Weiss (1981). It is interesting that empirical inquiry as hypotheses seeking is the view held by both Friedman and the NBER in the Koopmans-Vining debate. See the section on criticisms of the econometric approach in Chapter 3.

model is structural if its equations are strictly linked to the deep parameters of state variables. Sims, not satisfied with this conception of structure, reemphasizes the relative nature of structure.

Second, Sims's relativistic definition of structure seems to reflect his pragmatist methodology. He thinks that "a true probability model does not exist. Even in natural sciences, if one really looks close enough, there is no such thing and none of the models can be judged as really objective" (Sims, 1982b, p. 332). In other words, "despite the way we sometimes talk and write, we do not estimate parameters which define the truth" (p. 335). This view, which negates the possibility of constructing universally true models, seems to guarantee Sims's preference of the atheoretical approach to econometric inquiry. Then what is the criterion for judging the scientificity or objectivity of econometrics if the truth does not provide a foundation to econometric models? Sims (1982b) suggests that "econometrics can at least be much more scientific if it grounds its models more closely on the aspects of prior beliefs which economists and users of our analysis really do have in common" (p. 327). Practical usefulness would be one of the criteria for determining the scientific legitimacy of econometrics, and common sense suggests that the usefulness of econometric modeling lies in policy analysis or forecasting the effects of policy. Therefore, if a true econometric model does not exist and if a criterion for appraising models is forecasting performance, returning to the issue of defining structure it can be said that whether a model is structural depends on the use to which it is to be put – that is, on its forecasting performance. And "loosely restricted multivariate time series models," or VAR models, "though often labeled non-structural, are for practical purposes structural when the object is forecasting" (p. 332).

Sims's methodological position shares important similarities with both the NBER's empiricist and Friedman's instrumentalist methodologies. Whereas his underlying belief that an atheoretical, empiricist approach is capable of uncovering empirical regularities without the help of *a priori* economic theory parallels the NBER approach, his conviction that fore-casting performance is a criterion for judging econometric models is analogous to Friedman's methodology, in which prediction is suggested to be the only criterion for discriminating among different theories.

Hendry and the progressive research strategy in econometrics

The EBCT's econometrics strategy and Sims's atheoretical approach must be recognized as major trends in contemporary macroeconometrics, as must Leamer's (1978, 1983) influential criticism of the conventional practice of specification search. In addition to these currents is Hendry's econometric program. Since it has been developed largely within the tradition of British econometrics and has received little attention from American academics, there would be no point in trying to evaluate Hendry's program in the context of the development of American macroeconometrics. Whereas in the United States, Lucas's critique of econometric policy evaluation has had an enormous influence on macroeconometrics, Hendry's program in England has nothing to do with such recent American events. Rather, his program seems to be a natural outgrowth of the self-criticism of traditional econometric practices.

Hendry's "progressive research strategy" begins with the fundamental assumption of the "data generating process"[12] (DGP). The DGP is by definition a true characterization of the economic system, although unknowable, and the observed data are assumed to be uniquely generated by this process. A major role of economic theory can be conceived of as reducing the complex DGP to a simplistic form. The simplified DGP, however, is not ready for direct estimation. There remain such econometric problems as "the scale of the model and the paucity of the available observations" (Hendry, 1980, p. 400). Therefore, the derivation of a tangible econometric model from the DGP is not an obvious process, but a creative process that lies in the realms of art and psychology.

The recognition that the DGP is in principle unknowable and that the creation of econometric models is subjective and even whimsical leads Hendry to a clear distinction between the context of discovery and the context of justification.[13] As far as the context of discovery is concerned, "no single approach [to developing empirical models] is likely to be universally valid due to the manifest fact that we do not yet fully understand the world, and until we do, we cannot know what would have been the 'best' way to study it – even if a 'best' way were to exist" (Hendry and Mizon, 1985, p. 16). Hence, the reduction of the DGP to empirical models, or the process of discovery, is not a main concern of Hendry's progressive research strategy in econometrics.

It is in the context of justification, however, that econometrics can achieve scientific progress. "The three golden rules of econometrics are test, test and test. . . . Rigorously tested models, which adequately described the available data, encompassed previous findings and were

---

[12] For a formal definition of the DGP, see Hendry and Richard (1982, 1983).

[13] Note that "the context of discovery" and "the context of justification" are terms frequently used in the philosophy of science. It is one of Hendry's characteristics that he draws many ideas from this literature. Hendry (1980), for example, contrasts his econometric program with the Lakatosian "scientific research program." See also Hendry and Mizon (1985), where the distinction between the context of discovery and that of justification is a central concept.

derived from well based theories would greatly enhance any claim to be scientific" (Hendry, 1980, p. 403). In other words, an empirical model is scientific if it is consistent with both theoretical and empirical evidence and thus can systematically demonstrate its value, and not because it represents the DGP. In Hendry's (1983a) words:

A useful model must account for the observed past data, for current and continuing future data, for other models' findings, for other relevant evidence and be related to a consistent theory. Models satisfying all these requirements . . . can be used *as if* they constituted a data generation process even though successive encompassing models with smaller innovation variances will be developed over time. (p. 74)

The strategy and tactics of building models that fulfill a certain set of criteria comprise what Hendry calls the "progressive research strategy." Clearly recognizing econometric modeling "as a matter of design (like bridge building) not of garnering 'truth' (like an exercise in quantitative logic)" (Hendry and Mizon, 1985, p. 5), he suggests a set of design criteria: A model is called *congruent* if it is encompassing, data coherent, theory consistent, and data admissible and has constant parameters.[14] A congruent model can be temporarily accepted and used as if it were the DGP. Each of the design criteria can be explained as follows.[15]

A model should be *data coherent* in the sense that it adequately characterizes the past data at hand. This requires a regression residual to be white noise. In other words, the differences between the fitted values and the actual values should be random, so that the residual is not predictable from its own past alone. The presence of serial correlation in a model, for example, directly implies a systematic lack of fit. Conventionally, serial correlation is checked for by the Durbin–Watson statistic and then corrected for by a Cochrane–Orcutt transformation. According to Hendry, this conventional procedure is inadequate. Because the presence of serial correlation means that some systematic part of the residual is left unexplained, what is required in this case is a respecification of the model, not a reestimation like the Cochrane–Orcutt transformation. To test a null hypothesis of no serial correction, Hendry recommends the use of Lagrange multiplier tests.[16]

---

[14] In Hendry (1983) and Hendry and Richard (1983), "valid conditioning" or "weakly exogenous" is treated as a separate design criterion, whereas in Hendry and Mizon (1985) this criterion is included in data coherency. Here the former classification is adopted.

[15] For a more specific explanation of Hendry's design criteria, see Hendry (1983a, b) and Hendry and Richard (1983).

[16] Engle (1982) provides a complete discussion of Lagrange multiplier tests and their possible applications.

Regressors in a satisfactory model should be at least *weakly exogenous*.[17] Regressors are strongly exogenous if they are weakly exogenous and no feedback occurs. Whereas strong exogeneity is required for the purpose of forecasting, weak exogeneity would be sufficient for most inference purposes.

A model must show *parameter constancy*. This criterion requires the model to yield the same parameter values when applied outside the sample period. In practice, tests of parameter constancy can be carried out by reserving a number of observations at the end of the sample period for testing the forecasting accuracy of the estimated model. A Chow test would be appropriate here.

A model must be *data admissible*. "A model is data admissible if its fitted and forecasted values automatically satisfy the properties of the measurement system" (Hendry and Mizon, 1985, p. 7). The unemployment rate, for example, is positive and less than 100%; so the estimated unemployment rate should be consistent with such definitional constraints.

A model has to be *consistent with theory*. It is desirable that the model be constructed on the ground of the best available economic theory. This, of course, is not always the case, but a satisfactory model should be consistent with at least one among alternative theories.

Most important, a successful model should *encompass* rival models. A model that can account for the results obtained by rival models is said to be encompassing. It is variance encompassing if the model can explain the error variance of the rival, and it is parametric encompassing if it can explain all the parameters of the rival. Variance encompassing can be tested for by means of likelihood ratio tests, and parametic encompassing by means of a Wald test. Hendry considers this encompassing criterion to be an essential component of his progressive research strategy in econometrics.

To reiterate, when a model satisfies the six criteria delineated above, it is called congruent. Here it should be noted that since "a model is a constructed entity, rather than a facsimile of 'reality,'" what can be examined is its congruence not with reality, but "with our perceptions of that reality" (Hendry, 1984, p. 334). The informational sources of our perceptions include past data, contemporaneous data, future data, theory information, measurement information, and rival models. In this context, if there is no consensual perception of reality among researchers, the resulting model evaluations cannot, of course, be in agreement. In particular two different theories might end up with two different model

---

[17] For a statistical definition of weak exogeneity, see Engle, Hendry, and Richard (1983).

evaluations. This explains in part Hendry's reluctance to rely entirely on one particular theory. He believes that dynamic and macroeconomic theories are less than perfect and that only static microeconomic theories are reliable, since the latter represent the least disputable economic knowledge among economists. Nor does he accept the rational expectations hypothesis as valid theory. Hendry's attitude toward theory seems to be a middle road between the two extremes of Sims's atheoretical approach and the EBCT's econometric strategy.

CHAPTER 6

Conclusion

This book is a historical investigation of the theoretical development of equilibrium business cycle theory (EBCT). The approach to the setting of the problem is retrospective. In adopting this sort of approach, one takes the risk of selecting and interpreting historical materials unobjectively, thereby creating a distorted picture of history. However, when carefully applied, the retrospective approach has certain advantages. It involves comparisons of the past and the present, though its viewpoint is that of the latter. The similarities and dissimilarities thus uncovered would contribute to our understanding of the intrinsic characteristics of both the past and present. Three retrospective questions form the main thread of this book: How does economists' understanding of the business cycle in the past differ from that of contemporary thinkers? What sorts of theoretical momentum from the past have brought forth the current mode of understanding the cycle? And how have the relationships among cycle theory, classical economic theory, and empirical inferences evolved over time? In a sense, this book is an effort to provide a dialogue between past theoretical achievements and today's economic thinking.

As discussed in the preceding chapters, two central features of the EBCT are the optimization foundation and its econometric strategy. The optimization foundation suggests that economic phenomena should be viewed as outcomes of individuals' optimizing behaviors and thus that the business cycle has to be explained in terms of such behaviors. That is, one facet of the optimization foundation is that business cycles are understood to be equilibrium phenomena in which agents optimize and markets clear. The econometric strategy of the EBCT emphasizes the role of theory in empirical inquiry. This strategy requires econometric models to be explicitly derived from theoretical propositions. Hence, theoretical restrictions act as a bridge linking econometric models and *a priori* theory. Moreover, when equilibrium theory in conjunction with the rational expectations hypothesis is employed as the source of theoretical restrictions, those restrictions, called cross-equation restrictions, become the basis of Lucas's critique of econometric policy evaluation. This indicates that the success of conventional econometric models critically depends on ad hoc restrictions without theoretical grounds and that if such ad hoc restrictions are replaced by cross-equation restrictions, conventional models become useless in policy evaluation.

A main purpose of this book has been to investigate historically these two central features of the EBCT. First, the EBCT's view of business cycles, the equilibrium approach, has never been a dominant view in the long history of cycle theory. A natural question in this context is, Why did past business cycle theories in general deny the equilibrium approach as a basis of explaining cycles, or what are the underlying reasons for the irreconcilable cleavage between cycle theories and classical theory? Another question is related to the historical comparison between the equilibrium approach of the past and today's EBCT. Comparing two different bodies of theory that adopt ostensibly the same approach to the same problem would seem to be worthwhile. Second, the EBCT's econometric strategy in principle is not different from the Cowles Commission method. Both emphasize the role of *a priori* theory in empirical inquiry. In would thus seem to be of interest to investigate the historical process by which the Cowles Commission method was established. In the early history of the econometric movement, however, there were several criticisms of this method. The EBCT's econometric strategy, a child of the Cowles Commission method, has also been confronted by methodological criticisms and alternatives. This situation parallels the Cowles Commission's and might shed some light on the fundamental nature of empirical inquiry. Third and most important, a distinctive characteristic of the EBCT is that its econometric inferences are firmly incorporated in theory. This is quite remarkable if one recalls that, until the Second World War, business cycle theories and empirical business cycle analyses were two different subjects, carried out by two different groups of researchers using two different methodologies. A question in this connection is, What theoretical momentum in the history of cycle theories underlies the incorporation of descriptive cycle theory and econometric inquiry?

The main purpose of the book has been to examine these questions historically, and the following is a summary of the main insights that have emerged.

1. The tradition of business cycle theory was maintained mainly on the Continent, whereas in England cyclical fluctuations were not seriously studied within the discipline of classical economics until the turn of the century. In the Continental tradition, business cycles were perceived largely as being caused by fundamental contradictions inherent in the capitalist market system, reflecting the influence of Marxist economics. That is, Continental cycle theorists considered cycles to be endogenous to the market system. In England, however, although the cycle was not

seriously discussed, there was a tendency to explain it as a mere reflection of shocks external to the market system. In both traditions, classical economics, the main concern of which was to discover fundamental laws of prices and value, was considered to be irrelevant to discussions of business cycles. The interwar years, however, saw a genuine effort to incorporate the business cycle into classical doctrine. That effort was made by Hayek.

Hayek understood cycles to be consequences of individuals' mistaken decisions, caused by misleading price information, which was in turn triggered by monetary disturbances. Hayek's theory of the cycle is in many respects a predecessor of today's EBCT. Methodological individualism, the centrality of price mechanism as the information carrier, monetary disturbance as a source of cyclical fluctuations – these ideas, which are significant in Hayek's theory, also occupy an important part of the EBCT. The differences between them are not insignificant, however. Whereas Hayek portrays the path of business cycles as an "equilibrating" process, in the EBCT the path is conceived as a continuum of equilibrium. Moreover, Hayek's theory emphasizes "maladjustment in capital goods" in explaining the propagating effect of monetary disturbances on the market system. In the EBCT, however, there is no explicit capital theory to account for the propagating effect. In this regard, recent real business cycle theories, furthering the original framework of the EBCT, have reintroduced rich interwar-period discussions of the maladjustment of capital goods. This, however, seems to invite a new difficulty, for *money* comes to be unnecessary for real business cycle theory's explanation of the cycle, whereas the proposition that money is of no importance would be almost unacceptable to New Classical economists. Thus, there are elements of Hayek in both the EBCT and real business cycle theory, but this implies the disintegration of what for Hayek was a coherent program of research.

2. The early development of econometrics, which eventually led to the Cowles Commission method, basically followed two courses: empirical demand analysis and empirical business cycle analysis. Through the course of demand analysis, economic statisticians began to recognize the simultaneous relationships among economic variables and the need to introduce extra information for the identification of such relationships. That is to say, in the course of attempts to measure demand curves, the idea of "structure" and the associated "identification problem" were recognized, though not clearly, as basic conceptual issues in empirical inference. Another route, empirical business cycle analysis, was initially concerned with statistical descriptions of characteristics of cycles and their decomposition. Since Frisch articulated his scheme of distinguishing the propagation mechanism from external shocks, however, empirical business cycle analysis has tended to move away from the statistical description of cycles toward

the econometric approach, in which the emphasis is on the estimation of the coefficients in the structure or the propagation mechanism.

It was the Cowles Commission that provided some conceptual clarification of the diverse previous studies on the subject. By accepting both classical sampling theory and Frisch's scheme, the commission suggested structural-equation estimation as a legitimate method of econometrics. At the same time, such statistical tools as the maximum likelihood estimator and the LIML estimator, and the statistical properties of those estimators, which were closely associated with the structural-equation estimation, were also developed. Opponents of the Cowles Commission method, however, argued that the "structure" constructed by the method was not a true structure. Instead, they opted for a limited role for econometrics – one of statistical description and hypothesis seeking. This skepticism about the construction of true econometric structures also seems to form the core of contemporary criticism of the EBCT.

3. Looking back at the history of both cycle theory and econometrics, one sees that Frisch's scheme provided the theoretical impetus for important events in both cases. His distinction between the propagation mechanism and shocks implies that the conventional notion of the cycle defined in terms of periodicity, amplitude, and turning point can be theoretically described by a couple of stochastic difference equations. It follows that, if one could statistically construct those stochastic difference equations, or the propagation mechanism, there would be no reason for bothering with the conventional analysis. In this regard, Frisch's scheme is a key conception that made it possible to translate descriptive interwar-period cycle theory into econometric language.

Put somewhat differently, this scheme seems to be a predecessor of the contemporary mode of modeling business cycles as a system of stochastic difference equations, there being no explicit attempt to explain turning points and periodicity. Comparing contemporary with interwar cycle theories, it can be seen that the research direction has shifted from an explanation of the descriptive characteristics of cycles to the estimation and interpretation of the coefficients in a structural-equation system. It seems, therefore, that Frisch's scheme in some way was significant in changing the concept of cycles – from the cycle understood in terms of its descriptive characteristics to the cycle perceived simply as a special case of economic fluctuations. In other words, the very meaning of the word "cycle", the wavelike characteristics of economic time series, has come to have less importance.

Viewed in this way, the change in the concept of cycles and the related shift in research direction perhaps accounts to some degree for the sudden decline of interwar cycle theories. The theoretical impetus underlying these events seems to be Frisch's scheme.

An appraisal: style or content?

The main concern of this book has been to investigate the central features of the EBCT in a historical context, and in principle there has been no attempt to offer a detailed appraisal of the EBCT. As a way of concluding the study, however, this section draws a picture, albeit an incomplete one, of the EBCT from a methodological perspective in association with current macroeconomic thinking.

Theoreticians whose basic interests lie in the substantive content of the EBCT tend to point out that the EBCT has grown up on the foundation of monetarism, emphasizing that these two different bodies of theory have essentially the same outlook on economy, policy suggestions, and monetary theory. Thus, Tobin (1981) understands the EBCT to be the second monetarist counterrevolution. Laidler (1982) also places the EBCT in the intellectual tradition of Austrian economics and monetarism. What these theoreticians modestly suggest is that, as far as its theoretical content is concerned, the EBCT cannot be called revolutionary because it comprises at most extensions and refinements of the central themes of monetarism.

As a methodologist, Klamer (1981, 1984) supports this view. Klamer's methodological position negates the prevailing positivist philosophy of science, according to which scientific progress is achieved through an endless process of confrontations with the empirical world. In place of the positivist doctrine, he proposes the diversity of styles of argument in intellectual discourse, leading him to focus on the rhetorical or communicative aspects of science and consequently to deemphasize the substantive content of discourse such as theoretical claims and empirical evidence. When Klamer examines the case for viewing New Classical economics as an art of persuasion rather than a positive science, he concludes that "the distinctive claim of new classical economics would concern style, not substance (Klamer, 1984, p. 239). In recognition of this, New Classical economists like Lucas and Sargent manifest a new style of argument in their firm adherence to the optimization modeling strategy, which necessitates a full use of mathematical and statistical language. If this strategy alone is the distinctive feature of the EBCT and if its substantive content is simply a reaffirmation of the central themes of monetarism, then a natural conclusion would be that the EBCT represents a revolution in the style of argument, not in its content.

The issue, however, is not so simple. Philosophically one cannot presuppose that style or form is completely separable from content. Style and content are closely interconnected. New technological tools enable researchers to address new sets of problems and expand the scope of discourse in a particular direction. At the same time they also alter some key concepts, which previously were taken as a matter of course. When the style of argument is transformed and the old theoretical content is to be molded into a new form, there should be serious tensions between them. Conventional notions should be transformed, some content of the conventional theory lost, some new content added, and eventually a completely different way of looking at the phenomena shaped.[1]

Viewed in this way, the EBCT's firm adherence to the optimization modeling strategy not only is a technical turn in the style of argument, but also causes changes in its substantive content.[2] The style and substance complement each other. Compared with monetarism, this modeling strategy or theorizing principle forces the EBCT to simplify its theoretical ideas, so that the theory of money is reduced to a simple version of quantity theory and the conception of dynamic adjustment is simply discredited. It also allows the proponents of the EBCT to resolve the microfoundation problem, which was a painful theoretical dilemma for both Keynesians and monetarists.

Moreover, the adoption of this principle as an econometric strategy seems to further the Cowles Commission's method of simultaneous-equation estimation. As discussed in previous chapters, the spirit behind the Cowles Commission method was an endeavor to bridge economic theory and the empirical world, in which theoretical restrictions played the role of gearwheel. Although the Cowles Commission did not succeed at its own task, owing partly to a dubious conceptualization of econometric structure and partly to the lack of decisive statistical tools for testing competing theories, the EBCT's optimization econometric strategy settles the Cowles Commission's problem by forcing one to derive cross-equation restrictions from the optimizing behavior of individuals, thus ensuring the stability of econometric structure with respect to environmental changes like policy shifts. In this way, the EBCT's theorizing principle of optimization incorporates two virtually distinct fields, macroeconomic theory and econometrics, making the word "macroeconometrics" more plausible.

---

[1] Weintraub (1986) examines the shift in the meaning of equilibrium from market balance of forces to coordination, applying the Wittgensteinian language game idea. He suggests that the momentum of the conceptual shift is linked to the use of a mathematical proof strategy that depends on the fixed-point theorem, namely, that the mathematization of equilibrium analysis, a change in the style of argument, is responsible for this shift.

[2] Howitt (1986) also holds that the modeling strategy of New Classical economists "has a great deal of substantive content as a matter of practice" (p. 108), such as a view of the business cycle that is completely different from Keynesians' and different policy implications.

The somewhat controversial style of argument of New Classical economics, equipped with new technical language, redirects and redefines the scope of discourse. Its challenge, however, seems to be seriously restricted by computational and other technical factors.

References

Adelman, I., and Adelman, F. L., "The Dynamic Properties of the Klein-Goldberger Model." *Econometrica 27,* 1959, pp. 596-625.

Aftalion, A., "La réalité des surproductions générales." *Revue d'Economie Politique 12-13,* 1908-9, pp. 696-706; also pp. 81-117, 201-29, 241-59.

"The Theory of Economic Cycle Based on the Capitalistic Technique of Production." *Review of Economic Statistics 9,* 1927, pp. 165-70.

Allen, R. G. D., "The Assumptions of Linear Regression." *Economica 6* (N.S.), 1939, pp. 191-204.

Ames, E., "A Theoretical and Statistical Dilemma - The Contributions of Burns, Mitchell and Frickey to Business-Cycle Theory." *Econometrica 16,* 1948, pp. 347-69.

Anderson, E. E., "Further Evidence on the Monte Carlo Cycle in Business Activity." *Economic Inquiry 15,* 1977, pp. 269-76.

Anderson, T. W., and Rubin, H., "Estimation of the Parameters of a Single Equation in a Complete System of Stochastic Equations." *Annals of Mathematical Statistics 20,* 1949, pp. 46-63.

Barro, R., "Unanticipated Monetary Growth and Unemployment in the United States." *American Economic Review 67,* 1977, pp. 101-15.

"Unanticipated Money, Output, and the Price Level in the United States." *Journal of Political Economy 86,* 1978, pp. 549-80.

"The Equilibrium Approach to Business Cycles." In *Money, Expectations, and Business Cycles.* New York: Academic Press, 1981, pp. 41-78.

Begg, D. K. H., *The Rational Expectations Revolution in Macroeconomics.* Baltimore: Johns Hopkins University Press, 1982.

Black, F., "The ABCs of Business Cycles." *Financial Analysts Journal 37,* 1981, pp. 75-80.

"General Equilibrium and Business Cycles." Working Paper, National Bureau of Economic Research, New York, 1982.

Blanchard, O. J., and Watson, M. W., "Are Business Cycles all Alike?" Working Paper, National Bureau of Economic Research, New York, 1984.

Blatt, J. M., "On the Econometric Approach to Business-Cycle Analysis." *Oxford Economic Papers 30,* 1978, pp. 292-300.

"On the Frisch Model of Business Cycles." *Oxford Economic Papers 32,* 1980, pp. 467-79.

Dynamic Economic System: A Post-Keynesian Approach. Armonk, N.Y.: Sharpe, 1983.

Blaug, M., *Economic Theory in Retrospect,* 4th ed. Cambridge University Press, 1985.

Bleaney, M. F., *Underconsumption Theories: A History and Critical Analysis.* New York: International Publishers, 1976.

Boehm, S., "Time and Equilibrium: Hayek's Notion of Intertemporal Equilibrium Reconsidered." Paper presented at the History of Economics Society Annual Meetings, 1985.

Bronfenbrenner, M., *Is the Business Cycle Obsolete?* New York: Wiley, 1969.

Burns, A. F., and Mitchell, W. C., *Measuring Business Cycles.* New York: National Bureau of Economic Research, 1946.

Butos, W. N., "Hayek and General Equilibrium Analysis." *Southern Economic Journal 52,* 1985, pp. 332–43.

Carr, E. H., *What is History?* New York: Random House, 1961.

Christ, C. F., "A Test of an Econometric Model for the United States, 1921–1947." In *Conference on Business Cycles,* ed. G. Haberler. New York: National Bureau of Economic Research, 1951, pp. 35–106.

"History of the Cowles Commission, 1932–1952." In *Economic Theory and Measurement: A Twenty Year Research Report, 1932–1952.* Chicago: Cowles Commission for Research in Economics, 1952.

"Aggregate Econometric Models." *American Economic Review 46,* 1956, pp. 385–408.

"Econometrics in Economics: Some Achievements and Challenges." *Australian Economic Papers 6,* 1967, pp. 155–70.

Collard, D. A., "Pigou on Expectations and the Cycle." *Economic Journal 93,* 1983, pp. 411–14.

Cooley, T. F., and LeRoy, S. F., "Atheoretical Macroeconometrics: A Critique." *Journal of Monetary Economics 16,* 1985, pp. 283–308.

DeLong, J. B., and Summers, L. H., "Are Business Cycles Symmetric?" Working Paper, National Bureau of Economic Research, New York, 1984.

Doan, T., Litterman, R., and Sims, C. A., "Forecasting and Conditional Projection Using Realistic Prior Distributions." *Econometric Review 3,* 1984, pp. 1–100.

Eisenhart, C., "The Interpretation of Certain Regression Methods and Their Use in Biological and Industrial Research." *Annals of Mathematical Statistics 10,* 1939, pp. 162–86.

Engle, R. F., "A General Approach to Lagrange Multiplier Model Diagnostics." *Journal of Econometrics 20,* 1982, pp. 83–104.

Engle, R. F., Hendry, D. F., and Richard, J.-F., "Exogeneity." *Econometrica 51,* 1983, pp. 277–304.

Fisher, I., "Our Unstable Dollar and the So-Called Business Cycle." *Journal of the American Statistics Association 23,* 1925, pp. 179–202.

The Theory of Interest. New York: Macmillan, 1930.

Friedman, M., "Review of *Business Cycles in the United States of America, 1919–1932* by J. Tinbergen." *American Economic Review 30,* 1939, pp. 657–60.

"Comment." In *Conference on Business Cycles,* ed. G. Haberler. New York: National Bureau of Economic Research, 1951, pp. 107–14.

"The Methodology of Positive Economics." In *Essays in Positive Economics.* University of Chicago Press, 1953, pp. 3–46.

"The Role of Monetary Policy." *American Economic Review 58,* 1968, pp. 1–17.

Friedman, M., and Schwartz, A., *A Monetary History of the United States.* Princeton, N.J.: Princeton University Press, 1963a.

"Money and Business Cycles." *Review of Economics and Statistics 45,* (suppl.), 1963b.

Friedman, R. D., "Milton Friedman: Husband and Colleague." *Oriental Economist 44,* 1976, pp. 18–22.

Frisch, R., "Propagation Problems and Impulses Problems in Dynamic Economics." In *Economic Essays in Honor of Gustav Cassel.* London: Allen & Unwin, 1933, pp. 171–205.

Statistical Confluence Analysis by Means of Complete Regression Systems. Oslo: University Economics Institute, 1934a.

"More Pitfalls in Demand and Supply Curve Analysis." *Quarterly Journal of Economics 48,* 1934b, pp. 749–55.

Geweke, J., "Testing the Exogeneity Specification in the Complete Dynamic Simultaneous Equation Model." *Journal of Econometrics 7,* 1978, pp. 163–85.

"Macroeconometric Modelling and the Theory of the Representative Agent." Working Paper, Duke University, Durham, N.C., 1984.

Gilboy, E. W., "The Leontief and Schultz Methods of Deriving 'Demand' Curves." *Quarterly Journal of Economics 45,* 1931, pp. 218–61.

Gordon, R. A., "Business Cycles in the Interwar Period: The 'Quantitative-Historical' Approach." *American Economic Review, Papers and Proceedings 39,* 1949, pp. 47–63.

Gordon, R. J., "Output Fluctuations and Gradual Price Adjustment." *Journal of Economic Literature 19,* 1981, pp. 493–530.

Gordon, R. J., and King, S. E., "Output Cost of Disinflation in Traditional and Vector Autoregressive Models." *Brookings Papers on Economic Activity,* 1982, pp. 205–44.

Granger, C. W., "The Typical Spectral Shape of an Economic Variable." *Econometrica 34,* 1966, pp. 150–61.

"Investigating Causal Relations by Econometric Models and Cross-Spectral Methods." *Econometrica 37,* 1969, pp. 424–38.

Grossman, H., "The Natural-Rate Hypothesis, the Rational Expectations Hypothesis, and the Remarkable Survival of Non-Market-Clearing Assumptions." In *Variability in Employment, Price and Money,* ed. K. Brunner and A. H. Meltzer. Amsterdam: North Holland, 1983, pp. 225–46.

"Policy, Rational Expectations, and Positive Economic Analysis." Working Paper, Brown University, Providence, R.I., 1984.

Grossman, S., and Weiss, L., "Heterogeneous Information and the Theory of the Business Cycle." *Journal of Political Economy 90,* 1982, pp. 699–727.

Haavelmo, T., "The Inadequacy of Testing Dynamic Theory by Comparing Theoretical Solutions and Observed Cycles." *Econometrica 8,* 1940, pp. 312–21.

"The Effect of the Rate of Interest on Investment: A Note." *Review of Economics and Statistics 23,* 1941, pp. 49–52.

"The Statistical Implications of a System of Simultaneous Equations." *Econometrica 11,* 1943, pp. 1–12.

"The Probability Approach in Econometrics." *Econometrica 12,* (suppl.), 1944.

Haberler, G., *Prosperity and Depression,* 4th ed. New York: Atheneum, 1963.

Hands, D. W., "Ad hocness in Economics and the Popperian Tradition." Paper presented at J.J. Klant Symposium, 1985.

Hansen, A. H., *Business Cycles and National Income.* New York: Norton, 1951.

Hansen, L. P., "Large Sample Properties of Generalized Method of Moments Estimator." *Econometrica 50,* 1982, pp. 1029–54.

Hansen, L. P., and Sargent, T. J., "Formulating and Estimating Dynamic Linear Rational Expectations Models." *Journal of Economic Dynamics and Control 2,* 1980, pp. 7–46.

"Linear Rational Expectations Models for Dynamically Interrelated Variables." In *Rational Expectations and Econometric Practice,* vol. 1, ed. R. E. Lucas and T. J. Sargent. Minneapolis: University of Minnesota Press, 1981, pp. 127–56.

"Instrumental Variables Procedures for Estimating Linear Rational Expectations Models." *Journal of Monetary Economics 9,* 1982, pp. 263–96.

Hansen, L. P., and Singleton, K. J., "Generalized Instrumental Variables Estimation of Nonlinear Rational Expectations Models." *Econometrica 50,* 1982, pp. 1269–86.

Harrod, R. F., "The Expansion of Credit in an Advancing Community." *Economica 1,* (N.S.), 1934, pp. 287–99.

Hawtrey, R. G., *Good and Bad Trade.* London: Constable, 1913.

Monetary Reconstruction. London: Longman Group, 1923.

"Review of Hayek's *Prices and Production.*" *Economica 12,* 1932, pp. 119–25.

The Gold Standard in Theory and Practice, 2d ed. London: Longman Group, 1947.

Hayek, F. A., "Money and Capital: A Reply." *Economic Journal 42,* 1932, pp. 237–49.

Monetary Theory and the Trade Cycle. London: Cape, 1933.

Prices and Production, enl. 2d ed. London: Routledge & Kegan Paul, 1935.

"Economics and Knowledge." *Economica 4* (N.S.), 1937, pp. 33-54.

"A Comment." *Economica 9* (N.S.), 1942, pp. 383-5.

"Price Expectations, Monetary Disturbances and Malinvestments." First published (in German) in the *Nationalökonomisk Tidskrift 73,* 1935; reprinted in *AEA Readings in Business Cycle Theory.* Philadelphia: Balkiston, 1944, pp. 350-65.

"The Use of Knowledge in Society." *American Economic Review 35,* 1945, pp. 519-30.

"Economic Thought: The Austrian School." In *International Encyclopedia of the Social Sciences,* ed. D. L. Sills. New York: Macmillan, 1968.

"Three Elucidations of the Ricardo Effect." *Journal of Political Economy 77,* 1969, pp. 274-85.

"Intertemporal Price Equilibrium and Movements in the Value of Money." Originally published (in German) in *Weltwirtschaftliches Archiv,* 1928; reprinted in McCloughry, R. (ed.), *Hayek - Money, Capital, and Fluctuations: Early Essays.* University of Chicago Press, 1984, pp. 71-117.

Hendry, D. F., "Econometrics: Alchemy or Science?" *Economica 47,* 1980, pp. 387-406.

"On Keynesian Model Building and the Rational Expectations Critique: A Question of Methodology." *Cambridge Journal of Economics 7,* 1983a, pp. 69-75.

"Econometric Modelling: The 'Consumption Function' in Retrospect." *Scottish Journal of Political Economy 30,* 1983b, pp. 193-220.

"Some Potential Developments in Time-Series Econometrics During the Next Five Years." *Journal of the Royal Statistical Society, 147* (ser. A), 1984, pp. 327-39.

Hendry, D. F., and Mizon, G. E., "Procrustean Econometrics: Or Stretching and Squeezing Data," CEPR Discussion Paper No. 68, 1985.

Hendry, D. F., and Richard, J.-F., "On the Formulation of Empirical Models in Dynamic Econometrics." *Journal of Econometrics 20,* 1982, pp. 3-33.

"The Econometric Analysis of Economic Time Series." *International Statistical Review 51,* 1983, pp. 111-63.

Hexter, M. B., *Social Consequences of Business Cycles.* New York: Houghton Mifflin, 1925.

Hicks, J. R., *Value and Capital,* 2d ed. New York: Oxford University Press, 1946.

A Contribution to the Theory of the Trade Cycle. New York: Oxford University Press, 1950.

"The Hayek Story." In *Critical Essays in Monetary Theory.* New York: Oxford University Press, 1967.

Hicks, J., "Equilibrium and the Trade Cycle." Originally published (in German) in *Zeitschrift für Nationalökonomie 4,* 1933; reprinted in *Economic Inquiry 18,* 1980, pp. 523-34.

Hirsch, A., and de Marchi, N., "Making a Case When Theory is Untestable: Friedman's Monetary History." Unpublished manuscript, Duke University, Durham, N.C., 1985.

Hoover, K. D., "Two Types of Monetarism." *Journal of Economic Literature 22,* 1984, pp. 58-76.

Howitt, P., "Conversations with Economists: A Review Essay." *Journal of Monetary Economics 18,* 1986, pp. 103-18.

Hutchison, T. W., "Expectation and Rational Conduct." *Zeitschrift für Nationalökonomie 8,* 1937, pp. 636-53.

A Review of Economic Doctrines; 1870-1929. New York: Oxford University Press, 1953.

Jevons, W. S., *Investigations in Currency and Finance.* New York: Macmillan, 1884.

Jones, E. D., *Economic Crises.* New York: Macmillan, 1900.

Kaldor, N., "Professor Hayek and the Concertina Effect." *Economica 9* (N.S.), 1942, pp. 359-82.

Kalecki, M., "A Macrodynamic Theory of Business Cycles." *Econometrica 3,* 1935, pp. 327-44.

Kalman, R. E., "Dynamic Econometric Models: A System-Theoretic Critique." In *New Quantitative Techniques for Economic Analysis,* ed. G. P. Szego. New York: Academic Press, 1982, pp. 19-28.

Kantor, B., "Rational Expectations and Economic Thought." *Journal of Economic Literature 17,* 1979, pp. 1422–41.

Karaken, J. H., and Wallace, N. (eds.), *Models of Monetary Economics.* Minneapolis, Minn.: Federal Reserve Bank of Minneapolis, 1980.

Keynes, J. M., "Professor Tinbergen's Method." *Economic Journal 49,* 1939, pp. 558–68.

"Comment." *Economic Journal 50,* 1940, pp. 154–6.

Essays in Biography. New York: Norton, 1951.

The Collected Writings of John Maynard Keynes, vol. 14. London: Royal Economic Society/ Macmillan, 1973.

King, R. G., and Plosser, C. I., "Money, Credit and Prices in a Real Business Cycle." *American Economic Review 74,* 1984, pp. 363–80.

Klamer, A., *Levels of Discourse in the New Classical Economics.* Doctoral dissertation, Duke University, Durham, N.C.: 1981.

Conversations with Economists. Totawa, N.J.: Rowman & Allandeld, 1984.

Klein, L. R., *Economic Fluctuations in the United States 1921–1941* (Cowles Commission Monograph 11). New York: Wiley, 1950.

Klein, L. R., and Goldberger, A. S., *An Econometric Model of the United States 1929–1952.* Amsterdam: North Holland, 1955.

Koopmans, T. C., "The Logic of Econometric Business-Cycle Research." *Journal of Political Economy 49,* 1941, pp. 157–81.

"Measurement without Theory." *Review of Economics and Statistics 29,* 1947, pp. 161–72.

"Identification Problems in Economic Model Construction." *Econometrica 17,* 1949, pp. 125–44.

"The Econometric Approach to Business Fluctuations." *American Economic Review, Papers and Proceedings 39,* 1949b, pp. 64–72.

"A Reply." *Review of Economics and Statistics 31,* 1949c, pp. 86–91.

"Comments." *Review of Economics and Statistics 34,* 1952, pp. 200–5.

"The Interaction of Tools and Problems in Economics." In *Three Essays on the State of Economic Science.* New York: McGraw-Hill, 1957, pp. 167–220.

Koopmans, T. C., and Barsch, A. F., "Selected Topics in Economics Involving Mathematical Reasoning." *SIAM Review 1,* 1959.

Koopmans, T. C., Rubin, H., and Leipnik, R. B., "Measuring the Equation Systems of Dynamic Economics." In *Statistical Inference in Dynamic Economic Models* (Cowles Commission Monograph 10), ed. T. C. Koopmans. New York: Wiley, 1950, pp. 53–237.

Kuznets, S., "On the Analysis of Time Series." *Journal of the American Statistics Association 23,* 1928, pp. 38–50.

"Equilibrium Economics and Business Cycle Theory." *Quarterly Journal of Economics 44,* 1930, pp. 381–415.

Kydland, F. E., and Prescott, E. C., "Rules Rather Than Discretion: The Inconsistency of Optimal Plans." *Journal of Political Economy 85,* 1977, pp. 473–91.

"Time to Build and Aggregate Fluctuations." *Econometrica 50,* 1982, pp. 1345–70.

Laidler, D., *Monetarist Perspectives.* Cambridge, Mass.: Harvard University Press, 1982.

Lakatos, I., "Falsification and the Methodology of Scientific Research Programmes." In *Criticism and the Growth of Scientific Knowledge,* ed. I. Lakatos and A. Musgrave. Cambridge University Press, 1970, pp. 91–196.

Latsis, S. J. (ed.), *Methods and Appraisal in Economics.* Cambridge University Press, 1976.

Leamer, E. E., *Specification Search: Ad Hoc Inference with Non-Experimental Data.* New York: Wiley, 1978.

"Let's Take the Con out of Econometrics." *American Economic Review 73,* 1983, pp. 31–43.

Leijonhufvud, A., *On Keynesian Economics and the Economics of Keynes.* New York: Oxford University Press, 1968.

120   **References**

Leontief, W., "Ein Versuch zur Statistischen Analyse von Angebot and Nachfrage." *Weltwirtschafliches Archiv 30,* 1929.

Litterman, R., "A Bayesian Procedure for Forecasting with Vector Autoregressions." Working Paper, Massachusetts Institute of Technology, Cambridge, 1980.

"Forecasting with Bayesian Vector Autoregressions: Four Years of Experience." Working Paper, Federal Reserve Bank of Minneapolis, 1984.

Litterman, R., and Weiss, L., "Money, Interest Rate and Output." Working Paper, Federal Reserve Bank of Minneapolis, 1981.

Long, J. B., Jr., and Plosser, C. I., "Real Business Cycles." *Journal of Political Economy 91,* 1983, pp. 39–69.

Lucas, R. E., "Some International Evidence on Output–Inflation Tradeoffs." *American Economic Review 63,* 1973, pp. 326–34.

"An Equilibrium Model of the Business Cycle." *Journal of Political Economy 83,* 1975, pp. 1113–44.

"Econometric Policy Evaluation: A Critique." In *The Phillips Curve and Labor Market,* ed. K. Brunner and A. H. Meltzer. Amsterdam: North Holland, 1976, pp. 19–46.

"Understanding Business Cycles." In *Stabilization of the Domestic and International Economy,* ed. K. Brunner and A. H. Meltzer. Amsterdam: North Holland, 1977, pp. 7–29.

"Methods and Problems in Business Cycle Theory." *Journal of Money Credit and Banking 12,* 1980, pp. 696–715.

Studies in Business-Cycle Theory. Cambridge, Mass.: MIT Press, 1981.

Lucas, R. E., and Prescott, E., "Investment Under Uncertainty." *Econometrica 39,* 1971, pp. 659–81.

Lucas, R. E., and Rapping, L. A., "Real Wages, Employment and Inflation." *Journal of Political Economy 77,* 1969, pp. 721–54.

Lucas, R. E., and Sargent, T. J., "After Keynesian Macroeconomics." In *After the Phillips Curve: Persistence of High Inflation and High Unemployment* (Conference Series 19). Federal Reserve Bank of Boston, 1978, pp. 49–72.

(eds.), *Rational Expectations and Econometric Practice,* 2 vols. Minneapolis: University of Minnesota Press, 1981.

McCulloch, J. H., "The Monte Carlo Cycle in Business Activity." *Economic Inquiry 13,* 1975, pp. 303–21.

Machlup, F., "Hayek's Contribution to Economics." In *Essays on Hayek,* ed. F. Machlup. New York: NYU Press, 1976, pp. 13–59.

Malthus, T. R., *Principles of Political Economy,* 2d ed. London: Pickering, 1836.

Mann, H. B., and Wald, A., "On the Statistical Treatment of Linear Stochastic Difference Equations." *Econometrica 11,* 1943, pp. 173–220.

Marget, A. W., *The Theory of Prices,* vol. 1. New York: Prentice-Hall, 1938.

Marschak, J., "Some Comments." *Quarterly Journal of Economics 48,* 1934, pp. 759–66.

"Economic Structure, Path, Policy, and Prediction." *American Economic Review, Papers and Proceedings 37,* 1947, pp. 81–4.

"Statistical Inference in Economics: An Introduction." In *Statistical Inference in Dynamic Economic Models* (Cowles Commission Monograph 10), ed. T. C. Koopmans. New York: Wiley, 1950.

Metzler, L. A., "The Assumptions Implied in Least Squares Demand Techniques." *Review of Economics and Statistics 22,* 1940, pp. 138–49.

Milgate, M., "On the Origin of the Notion of 'Intertemporal Equilibrium.' " *Economica 46,* 1979, pp. 1–10.

Mill, J. S., *Principles of Political Economy,* new ed., ed. W. J. Ashley. London: Longman Group, 1909.

Mills, F. C., "On Measurement in Economics." In *The Trend of Economics*, ed. R. G. Tugwell. New York: Knopf, 1924, pp. 51–3.

Mishkin, F. S., *A Rational Expectations Approach to Macroeconometrics: Testing Ineffectiveness and Efficient-Markets Models*. University of Chicago Press, 1983a.

"A Comment." In *Variability in Employment, Price and Money*, ed. K. Brunner and A. H. Meltzer. Amsterdam: North Holland, 1983b, pp. 247–52.

Mitchell, W. C., *Business Cycles*. Berkeley and Los Angeles: University of California Press, 1913.

Business Cycles: The Problem and Its Setting. New York: National Bureau of Economic Research, 1927.

What Happens During Business Cycles. New York: National Bureau of Economic Research, 1951.

Moore, H. L., *Economic Cycles: Their Law and Cause*. New York: Macmillan, 1914.

Morgenstern, O., "Perfect Foresight and Economic Equilibrium." First published (in German) in *Zeitschrift für Nationalökonomie 6*, 1935; reprinted in *Selected Economic Writings of Oskar Morgenstern*, ed. A. Schotter. New York: NYU Press, 1976, pp. 169–83.

Moss, L. S., and Vaughn, K. I., "Hayek's Ricardo Effect: A Second Look." *History of Political Economy 18*, 1986, pp. 545–65.

Muth, J. F., "Rational Expectations and the Theory of Price Movements." *Econometrica 29*, 1961, pp. 315–35.

Neftci, S. N., "Are Economic Time-Series Asymmetric Over the Business-Cycle?" *Journal of Political Economy 92*, 1984, pp. 307–28.

O'Driscoll, G. P., *Economics as a Coordination Problem*. Kansas City: Andrews & McMeel, 1977.

"Money: Menger's Evolutionary Theory." *History of Political Economy 18*, 1986, pp. 601–16.

O'Driscoll, G. P., and Rizzo, M. J., *The Economics of Time and Ignorance*. Oxford: Blackwell Publisher, 1985.

Persons, W. M., "The Correlation of Time Series." In *Handbook of Mathematical Statistics*, ed. H. L. Rietz. Cambridge, Mass.: Riverside Press, 1924.

Pheby, J., "Keynes on Econometrics." Mimeo, 1985.

Phelps, E. S., *Microeconomic Foundations of Employment and Inflation*. New York: Norton, 1970.

Pigou, A. C., *Industrial Fluctuations*. New York: Macmillan, 1927.

Rashid, S., "Malthus' Model of General Gluts." *History of Political Economy 9*, 1977, pp. 366–83.

Ricardo, D., *On the Principles of Political Economy and Taxation: The Works and Correspondence of David Ricardo*. vol. 1, ed. P. Sraffa and M. H. Dobb. Cambridge University Press, 1951.

Robertson, D. H., *Banking Policy and the Price Level*. London: King, 1926.

"Industrial Fluctuations and the Natural Rate of Interest." *Economic Journal 44*, 1934, pp. 650–6.

Roos, C. F., *Dynamic Economics*. Bloomington, Ind.: Principia Press, 1934.

"A General Invariant Criterion of Fit for Lines and Planes Where All Variables Are Subject to Error." *Metron 13*, 1937, pp. 3–20.

Rosenstein-Rodan, P. N., "The Role of Time in Economic Theory." *Economica 1* (N.S.), 1934, pp. 77–97.

Sargent, T. J., "A Classical Macroeconomic Model for the United States." *Journal of Political Economy 84*, 1976a, pp. 207–37.

"The Observational Equivalence of Natural and Unnatural Rate Theories of Macroeconomics." *Journal of Political Economy 84*, 1976b, pp. 631–40.

Macroeconomic Theory. New York: Academic Press, 1979.

"Interpreting Economic Time Series." *Journal of Political Economy 89*, 1981, pp. 213–48.

122   References

"Autoregressions, Expectations and Advice." *American Economic Review, Papers and Proceedings 74,* 1984, pp. 408–15.

Sargent, T. J., and Sims, C. A., "Business Cycle Modeling without Pretending to Have Too Much a Priori Economic Theory." In *New Methods in Business Cycle Reserch*, ed. C. A. Sims. Minneapolis, Minn.: Federal Reserve Bank of Minneapolis, 1977, pp. 45–109.

Sargent, T. J., and Wallace, N., "Rational Expectations, the Optimal Monetary Instrument and the Optimal Money Supply Rule." *Journal of Political Economy 83,* 1975, pp. 241–54.

Schultz, H., *Statistical Laws of Demand and Supply with Special Application to Sugar.* University of Chicago Press, 1928.

The Theory and Measurement of Demand. University of Chicago Press, 1938.

Schumpeter, J. A., *Business Cycles*, vol. 1, New York: McGraw-Hill, 1939.

History of Economic Analysis. New York: Oxford University Press, 1954.

Sheffrin, S. M., *Rational Expectations.* Cambridge University Press, 1983.

Simon, H. A., *The Sciences of the Artificial.* Cambridge, Mass.: MIT Press, 1969.

Sims, C. A., "Money, Income and Causality." *American Economic Review 62,* 1972, pp. 540–52.

"Exogeneity and Causal Ordering in Macroeconometric Models." In *New Methods in Business Cycle Research*, ed. C. A. Sims. Minneapolis, Minn.: Federal Reserve Bank of Minneapolis, 1977, pp. 23–43.

"Macroeconomics and Reality." *Econometrica 48,* 1980a, pp. 1–48.

"Comparison of Interwar and Postwar Business Cycles: Monetarism Reconsidered." *American Economic Review, Papers, and Proceedings 70,* 1980b, pp. 250–7.

"Policy Analysis with Econometric Model." *Brookings Papers on Economic Activity,* 1982a, pp. 107–52.

"Scientific Standards in Econometric Modeling." In *Current Development in the Interface: Economics, Econometrics, Mathematics*, ed. M. Mazewinkel and A. H. G. Rinnooy Kan. Dordrecht: Reidel, 1982b, pp. 317–40.

"Is There a Monetary Business Cycle?" *American Economic Review, Papers and Proceedings 73,* 1983, pp. 228–33.

Slutsky, E., "The Summation of Random Causes as the Source of Cyclic Process." *Econometrica 5,* 1937, pp. 105–46.

Sraffa, P., "Dr. Hayek on Money and Capital." *Economic Journal 42,* 1932, pp. 42–53.

Production of Commodities by Means of Commodities. Cambridge University Press, 1960.

Stigler, G. J., "The Limitations of Statistical Demand Curves." *Journal of the American Statistics Association 34,* 1939, pp. 469–81.

Tinbergen, J., *Statistical Testing of Business Cycle Theories*, 2 vols. Geneva: League of Nations, 1939.

Tintner, G., "A Note on Economic Aspects of the Theory of Errors in Time Series." *Quarterly Journal of Economics 53,* 1938, pp. 141–9.

Tobin, J., "Are New Classical Models Plausible Enough to Guide Policy?" *Journal of Money Credit and Banking 12,* 1980, pp. 788–99.

"The Monetarist Counter-revolution Today: An Appraisal." *Economic Journal 91,* 1981, pp. 29–42.

"Neoclassical Theory in America: J. B. Clark and Fisher." *American Economic Review 76* (suppl.), 1985, pp. 28–38.

Tugan-Baranovsky, M., *Les industrielles en Angleterre.* Paris, 1913.

Vining, R., "Koopmans on the Choice of Variables to be Studied and of Methods of Measurement." *Review of Economics and Statistics 31,* 1949a, pp. 77–94.

"A Rejoinder." *Review of Economics and Statistics 31,* 1949b, pp. 91–4.

Wald, A., "A Fitting of Straight Lines if Both Variables Are Subject to Error." *Annals of Mathematical Statistics 11,* 1940, pp. 284–300.

Weintraub, E. R., *General Equilibrium Analysis: Studies in Appraisal*. Cambridge University Press, 1985.

"On the Brittleness of the Orange Equilibrium." Unpublished manuscript, Duke University, Durham, N.C., 1986.

Wicksell, K., *Lectures on Political Economy*, 2 vols. New York: Macmillan, 1935.

Interest and Prices, trans. R. F. Kahn. New York: Macmillan, 1936.

Working, E. J., "What Do Statistical 'Demand Curves' Show?" *Quarterly Journal of Economics 41*, 1927, pp. 212–35.

Index

KIM: Equilibrium business cycle
theory = historical perspective *